James Francis Hadland was born just prior to World War II in Birmingham, England. He was educated at King Edwards School, obtaining O & A Levels and later BSc & MSc in engineering. After many years as an engineer and then a lecturer, depression crept insidiously into his life and full-time work became exceptionally difficult. Fortuitously there was an offer of early retirement and although his children were still at school, he accepted this and found some part-time employment.

Producing this book helped him enormously and he believes it has been of use to other sufferers. Recovery took time but eventually was complete.

James has also authored *The Answers to Every Problem. Yes, Every Last One*.

This book is dedicated entirely to its readers who may be afflicted by depression either directly themselves or because a loved one is suffering.

James Francis Hadland

Depression Due to Stress

Survival, Recovery, Prevention

AUSTIN MACAULEY PUBLISHERS™

LONDON • CAMBRIDGE • NEW YORK • SHARJAH

A CIP catalogue record for this title is available from the British Library.

ISBN 9781528901611 (Paperback)
ISBN 9781528957106 (ePub e-book)

www.austinmacauley.com

First Published (2021)
Austin Macauley Publishers Ltd
25 Canada Square
Canary Wharf
London
E14 5LQ

I acknowledge with deep gratitude the higher power which inspired and enabled me to write this book. Thank you to Teresa and Steve who read through the draft manuscript. Their comments were very helpful and much appreciated.

Table of Contents

Chapter 1   **11**

Introduction
    Symptoms of Depression

Chapter 2   **22**

A Few Words About Anxiety

Chapter 3   **26**

Causes of Depression

Chapter 4   **34**

The Underlying Origin of All Depression

Chapter 5   **39**

The History of a Particular Personal Depression

Chapter 6   **46**

The Inevitability of a Religious Aspect

Chapter 7   **52**

The Road to Recovery
    Part 1 – The Production of Written Records

Chapter 8   **67**

The Road to Recovery
    Part 2 – The Use of Written Records

Chapter 9   72

Using This Book as a Manual to Help Yourself
   General Thoughts

Chapter 10   76

Specific Suggestions to Assist You in Your Own Recovery or Prevention Programme

Chapter 11   99

A Few Thoughts for Those People Concerned About Someone Else with or Approaching Depression

Chapter 12   104

Final Summary
   Recommended Procedures When Reading Through This Book Again

Chapter 1

Introduction

Symptoms of Depression

This book is written by a sufferer of depression (and probably, anxiety) who is now on the road to recovery. It has four main purposes – (1) as a record of my own illness and eventually, complete recovery, (2) to get my brains moving again, (3) in the hope that it might be of some use to fellow sufferers and those that want to help them; and (4) as a means of prevention for those people who are drifting subconsciously down the path to depression.

I am not sure which is the principal reason. The first will certainly have a successful outcome because the finished work will be of use to me in the same way as my diary and journal are – helping me understand my problems. Of necessity my grey matter will be reactivated, so objective number two will also be met. If you read this right through, there is a very good chance that the third will also be worthwhile. I say this with confidence because there is nothing special about me. You and I are the same. If you have depression, it is the same as what I have. I am getting better, so you will get better. If you are concerned about someone else, then I expect this book to improve your understanding of the illness and thus, how you can help this other person to recover.

The following question has also crossed my mind several times – if I had known earlier what I know now, could the infirmity be prevented? The answer, from where I am now, is definitely *YES*. If you are partially down the road which I trod, and you take some notice of my signs and symptoms, then you can undoubtedly avoid a lot of grief yourself.

I have no medical qualifications at all. My working life has been spent in electrical engineering – initially as an apprentice, then as an engineer and finally as a lecturer in higher and further education. Nonetheless, I have gained experience of depression first hand, and my writing is qualified by this experience. However, since my health is not yet fully restored, this manuscript may not be constructed as well as I would have liked. For instance, there could be repetition of certain precepts because it is difficult for me to retain the whole text in my head. I cannot always remember if or when I made certain points, despite my copious notes and jottings.

There is no doubt in my mind that depression is the illness caused by our modern way of life in the same way as lung cancer is the illness resulting from smoking tobacco (speaking generally). Both can be equally fatal. Depression can be extremely serious and should be recognised as such. You cannot 'pull yourself together', as those who are healthy may tell you (or want to tell you even if they do not actually say it), any more than a person with cancerous lungs can 'snap out of it'. If you could, you would. The terminal condition for cancer can be death, and equally, this can be the terminal condition for untreated depression. It can be just as deadly as cancer.

You do not die directly of depression itself. It causes extremely negative feelings; it robs you of joy. If this continues over a long enough period of time, there can be thoughts of suicide, which the sufferer presumably considers to be the solution. We shall see later (Chapter 6) that this is definitely not the case. It would just exchange one set of problems for a different set. However, I personally knew an extremely charming person who took his own life as a result of depression. We were all totally amazed, you would never have suspected it, although those closer to him realised later that there had been warning signs. Unfortunately, his is by no means an isolated tragedy, but there is a vastly superior alternative.

Depression may not be obvious to the patient or to those around him or her. Lung cancer is fairly conspicuous – shadows on X-ray plates, coughing, weight loss, physical decay, etc. Depression can creep up unremarked and by the time it is recognised, the condition can already be serious. Also, you may have a doctor who subscribes to the 'we all have stress, you know' syndrome. This will merely delay diagnosis and make you think that perhaps you are causing an unnecessary fuss, as happened to me. (I emphasise that my present doctor is totally competent and caring and without her I would have been in very serious trouble. I am greatly in her debt.)

What are the symptoms of depression? I can relate mine and those I have observed in others. The list may not be exhaustive but I think it will encompass most of them. I am not sure whether these are indications of depression specifically, or are symptoms of stress. I suppose, in essence they are really manifestations of stress, which, if not treated, will inevitably lead to the dark melancholy, negative, joyless feelings, pervading most of your waking hours that constitute depression. It will not serve our cause, if we get bogged down in the fine points of medical jargon, so perhaps, we could bear in mind that we may be discussing stress or depression. If you are suffering from depression then you can expect to recognise these symptoms. If you have the symptoms (which almost certainly means you are under stress), but you are not yet in depression, then you will surely need remedial action so that you can avoid it.

1) *A feeling of being ill without any understanding of what it is:* You know how you have a feeling of well-being when life is good? This sensation is the exact opposite of that. It permeates everything you do. You become cheerless. It makes work a chore, and although I have always enjoyed my work, it was reduced to a duty to be endured.

2) *Over-reaction:* There might be a trivial family matter – a downstairs light is left on, all night. "What is the matter with you? Can't you switch anything off? Who do you think pays the bills? Do I have to watch everybody all the time?" It produces bad relationships at work, at home, wherever.

3) *Short-term memory loss:* This can become most frustrating. You need to commit everything to paper. Otherwise, if you leave the house to do (say) four things, you arrive in town and can only remember three of them. The time interval may only be a few minutes but you cannot recall the fourth item. Later in the day, when your spouse asks you for the stamps for the urgent letters, you know what it was. It makes you sloppy in life and inefficient in your job.

4) *Lack of enthusiasm:* You survive each day without much, if any, interest in it. You do what needs to be done and it is probably boring. You are glad that it is out of the way. You are not pleased with any achievement. You do not think, *I am really pleased with that. That is a real improvement. A good job, well done.*

5) *Tired:* During the day, perhaps mid-morning or early afternoon, there is a feeling of almost unbearable fatigue. If you are unable to have a sleep because you are at work, playgroup or caring for little ones, then you only just survive and the exhaustion results in a very short fuse. You tend to make mistakes and you are close to tears with frustration and weariness. When there is relief, you collapse in a chair to fall asleep for at least an hour, usually more. This makes you less effective in employment or motherhood and your day could have been much more productive than it was.

6) *Inward-looking:* You can only see your own problems, which are numerous. Events seem to be against you. You probably take everything personally. Nobody appears to care about your difficulties but they expect you to care about theirs. The paradox is that you may take an excessive interest in another's welfare in order to hide your own predicament. I know one dear lady who does this almost to the point of embarrassment. I am not sure why. Perhaps we depressives feel guilty about having such a 'silly' illness (silly as perceived by others).

7) *Easily discouraged:* You might think about going somewhere to get something for yourself. Immediately, everyone in the family wants to go somewhere different for something else. You just cannot be bothered to argue. "Forget it, I'm not bothered, anyway. You take the car; I'm going out for a walk." If there is any effort or persistence required to reach a goal (and probably a very modest one), the chances are that it will not be achieved. "I will do that sometime, but it won't be today."

8) *Easily overwhelmed:* Not quite the same as (7) above. Inevitably there are some tasks that are unavoidable – fetch the children, do the shopping, go to the doctor's, cook the meals, wash up, go to work, pay the bills, wash the clothes, etc. Equally inevitably, several essential duties will require attention almost simultaneously. You cannot see how you can cope with them all, in the time frame imposed on you. The tasks are probably simple but you do not know where to begin. You can feel the stress building up. Somehow you scrape through, most likely by neglecting or postponing one of the burdens which will cause you even more hassle tomorrow, but you do not care.

9) *Feel in need of help:* You wish that somebody would help you. As you see it, you are doing everything yourself and nobody cares. Other people seem to be getting along fine and only come to you when they have a problem. What you need is someone (preferably all-knowing and all-powerful with plenty of money and totally trustworthy) to say, "You have a rest; I will look after everything for you. I will deal with all your responsibilities, you need not do anything at all, until you feel better." If you are a manager or a parent, this is not a good leadership quality. It will make everything that much harder.

10) *Fitful sleep:* Before we had children, I used to have trouble getting off to sleep. I would lie awake for hours, half-tired but with my mind full of churning thoughts. My wife would sleep peacefully by my side, she had no trouble at all.

11) Our children cured my insomnia overnight, so to speak. The first had colic which lasted three months. He was also hyper- active and needed very little rest. Two more were born, giving us three under the age of four. They brought us total joy and corresponding exhaustion. For some six years, I never slept for more than two hours at a stretch, so when there was an opportunity, I was unconscious in an instant. As they grew up, I was able to sleep all night. It never took more than a few seconds after my head arrived on the pillow.

12) This was the case for many years. Then I began to wake several times during the night and had difficulty getting off again. In the morning the alarm would make me jump, whether I was sleeping or just dozing. Poor nights are bad news for the next day at work or parenting. I slept better at weekends, Friday particularly, and at the beginning of holidays.

13) *Slow to learn:* My work involved engineering – electrical, electronic, control and computing. Apart from materials technology, on which they depend and to which they are allied, nothing advances so quickly. This has its advantages, such as that you do not have time to become bored but it means that there is continual updating and learning.

14) During my undergraduate and graduate studies, I acquired knowledge and skills quite quickly. In the following 25 and more years, I kept pace with the technology and with the business of teaching, administration and management, which constituted my working life. I accomplished this without much effort or stress because I was well. I enjoyed my family, my career, my social and leisure life.

15) Then, there came a time when instead of understanding a new concept almost instantly and seeing the applications straight away, I was really struggling to discover what was going on. It could take hours or even days for these unfamiliar ideas to sink in. This leads to ineptitude in learning and time management, particularly at work.

16) *Yawn a lot:* The next three are physical manifestations similar to poor sleep. I would stagger out of bed in the morning and start yawning. I would yawn while shaving, having breakfast, making sandwiches, driving to work and at work. My colleagues commented on it. It seemed to be infectious. They yawned as well.

17) *Hands shake:* I would find that my hands shook involuntarily; not violently, but sufficiently to cause considerable difficulty when writing. Indeed, my handwriting has changed for the worse. It required some concentration to induce my hand to form the

letters. There is improvement now but it is still an effort.

18) *Intake of breath:* This is difficult to describe. When a child has been crying because of a mishap so that the distress lasts some time, there is an interval before complete recovery when there is an inward sob or sigh which occurs as the breath is sucked in. This occurs now and again, over a period of a few minutes, before the child returns to normal. I can remember this myself as an infant. It was now happening to me several times a day as an adult. It produces a feeling of deep sorrow.

19) *Solitary walking:* I needed to be outdoors in the daylight, preferably in the sunshine and to walk on my own. It was no good standing still or sitting down, I had to be moving even though the pace was usually slow. This was especially necessary after a stressful management meeting. Sometimes I had to leave the building even though it was not time for lunch. I always walked before work and in the lunch time, regardless of the weather, and often for a few minutes during tea break. It was a compulsion. I had to be outside and in solitude.

20) *Negative outlook:* You always have a reason why something cannot be done. If it can be done, then you know why you are not going to do it. You oppose any suggestions that are made to you. You dig in. Nobody is going to coerce you, even if it might be beneficial for you. You are stuck in the groove and that is where you are staying, thank you.

21) *'Nothing' feeling:* Sometimes I felt absolutely nothing – no anger, no pleasure, no desire to live, no desire to die, no concern, zero. It is very disturbing. You think that people are idiots when they drive

badly or make mistakes. You have no regard for people or things. If, for instance, someone was involved in an accident you would go and help, but you would not care if they were hurt. You read dreadful reports in the newspaper and you have no feelings about them. Fortunately, this did not occur often. It is a very weird sensation.

22) *Time-warp impression:* As you look back on the day and see yourself in various situations that you have been through, it is like a motion picture of someone else. You cannot believe it was you. It is not particularly unpleasant, just odd.

23) *Dithering:* When you have a small task to perform, it is very hard to get going. The upstairs window pane needs replacing. You need glass, putty and probably paint for the sill which is rotting. You just do not know where to start. Is there a pot of paint in the shed? Are the ladders still safe? Where did I put that sheet of glass, left over from the greenhouse? Who borrowed the glass cutters? You faff about not knowing what to buy or what order to tackle in each exercise and the whole job takes three times as long as it should. Frustration and fatigue lead to errors. The final result is unsatisfactory, but it will have to do.

Summary

The 23 features above (apart from no. 18 perhaps), may not be remarkable in themselves. I am sure they are exhibited at some point or another in all normal healthy people. I can recall having them on infrequent occasions all my life. When I expressed them to my doctor, I was suffering from all of them nearly all of the time. One or two, now and again may mean nothing; all of them, most of the time means depression induced by abnormal and prolonged stress – significant, deep-rooted depression – and hence, corrective action is vital. Some remedies and preventative prescriptions are discussed later.

At this point we are at the diagnosis stage only, we need more understanding before looking for solutions.

Chapter 2
A Few Words About Anxiety

Some years ago, (before I knew that I was ill), a friend of mine who suffered from severe depression told me that his doctor had also discussed the subject of anxiety with him. He was quite definite that the medical profession regards the two ailments as different, although I imagine that the symptoms probably overlap. There is no cause to become involved with semantics, but I thought it was worth acknowledging the differentiation made between the two. Personally, I do not think it is significant what name is given to the illness, the objective is to recuperate. Though I do feel that if your depression is severe, you are not bothered about getting better because you are not the slightest bit interested in anything.

During one of the 10 sessions of one-to-one counselling which I attended on the recommendation of my doctor, I asked my counsellor about the differences (real or apparent) between depression and anxiety. As I was seriously ill at the time and finding life generally monotonous, the question was rather academic but I thought I might as well be conversant with the terminology. The counselling turned out to be exceedingly helpful and we will return to this in detail in *Chapter 10*. From notes taken during the sessions recorded:

- Anxiety – more obvious as agitation.
- Depression – suppression of feelings.

The two most obvious indications of anxiety which I have noticed are:

- "Did I shut the front door?" syndrome
- Profuse sweating

I have suffered mildly from the first, and never from the second, except from normal physical exertion during ice hockey, indoor soccer etc., although I have overheated as a result of mental turmoil.

Checking the front door, house windows, gas fire, telephone etc., an absurd number of times is a habit so easy to pick up. I think the most I have done is five or so, but I understand it is possible to repeat the action so many times that you spend tens of minutes at it before you can escape. It is quite irrational. For me it is fading away as my recovery consolidates.

I knew two people who endured sudden attacks of copious sweating. It would come from nowhere. One of them would be sitting at his desk working away, and in seconds, he was soaked; all his clothes were drenched and he would have to go home and change. It was quite involuntary; he could do nothing about it. I believe that his domestic life was in disarray and he was looking after his two children of school age as a single parent. This put him in a state of emotional stress which I imagine was causing the depression as well. The last time we met he had successfully adjusted to his predicament and there was no more anxiety sweating.

I have a friend who has also suffered similar discomfort. He had earned and squandered a great deal of money and at the time was, near enough broke. This was especially hard for one who was accustomed to years of wealth. He too had family problems which, in his case, culminated in virtual isolation. He lived on his own in the middle of nowhere, with no transport and no bus service. His doctor had diagnosed depression and anxiety. He would prepare to go out and for no obvious reason would be covered in perspiration which would saturate his clothing. Although his financial affairs have not improved, family communication has, and the excessive sweating has got terminated.

I have personally but infrequently experienced a noticeable increase in body temperature as a consequence of emotional exertions, but the causes were evident. Two occasions come to my mind. In the first one, there was a waste of scarce resources (namely a camping gas bottle, almost empty) during a prolonged power cut. The gas was being used to boil water to fill a hot-water bottle instead of being saved for essential cooking. In the second case, I was seething over an obtrusive questionnaire which I was supposed to complete. Both instances were trivial. What caused my physical overheating was that I was being forced by circumstances to put up with them. This may have been anxiety but more likely just anger and frustration. Perhaps it is a mild condition which could be compounded if the source is a severe trauma rather than a frivolous event.

Summary

For what it is worth, anxiety is apparently considered by professionals as a separate medical issue. It might be a manifestation of depression. I do not believe that you can have life threatening anxiety in the same manner as you can with depression. I think that anxiety is a milder affliction but I emphasise that I am not qualified medically. My writing is from personal experience only.

Chapter 3
Causes of Depression

Back to depression then. The first line of the title of this book is what my doctor wrote on my sick note, and for sure, depression is caused by stress. Before investigating areas where stress originates, I would like to mention the physical aspect. During counselling, I asked about a prescription (tablets) which my doctor had recommended. I regard depression as a mental illness and I could not comprehend what these tablets would do or how they would work. I also enquired at four chemists. In my counselling notes, I had recorded:

"There is a physiological component in depression, e.g. women after childbirth, menopause, etc. This may be due to hormones. My prescription is chemical changes to the brain."

I never felt happy about the second medicine suggested. The first one had most peculiar side-effects and I discontinued it after a few days. Apparently, it takes two weeks before there is any noticeable benefit so I never had the opportunity to experience any. Since I definitely did not fancy having my brain changed, I never availed myself of the second at all. However, some people swear by their tablets and I am certainly not knocking prescriptions. Antibiotics, for instance, are most effective, but then I can visualise the battle of the microbes at the location of the infection. I just worry about antidepressants (probably a feature of the ailment), although I can understand the general concept behind them. If depression is considered to induce or to be induced by variations in the chemistry of the brain (I have no idea if this is the case), then it makes sense to try to stabilise these with suitable drugs (but they are not for me, thanks anyway).

While we are still discussing the physical side of depression, there is no doubt that fatigue can have a degenerative influence on us. We rarely feel good when we are tired. If you consider how much enthusiasm you have on a Friday evening after a long week at work (excluding any exceptional occasions when you are going away for a holiday) compared with how you feel on the following Saturday morning after a good night's sleep, with a whole weekend in front of you; it becomes manifest that our feelgood factor is dependent in some degree on our physical condition. Tiredness brought about by stress due to pressure from external factors, produces depression and anxiety.

Returning momentarily to the unusual Friday evening when something really stimulating or different is in the offing, we find that our interest overrides the weariness and we do not feel anywhere near so tired. While this is excellent in one way, it can be hazardous in another as the temporary enthusiasm for the different activity can cloak the depression. It is not a cure; it is a mask. This is amplified in a later chapter. This one, as we have already stated, pertains to causes of depression.

However, before moving on, I think that healthy fatigue is worth a few words. This occurs after participating in some physical activity in which you really revel, in my case ice skating or dinghy sailing, as you come back thoroughly enervated. You are just as tired in these circumstances as on the aforementioned Friday night, but you feel good. You struggle into bed thinking, I *really enjoyed that*, sleep solidly and wake refreshed despite some aches. Even these are pleasurable because they remind you of a good day. Although you were shattered, you have a feeling of well-being. In fact, I am stating the obvious that our physical situation has an impact on our mental welfare or as my counsellor said, there is a physiological factor in depression.

Currently we are discussing the causes of depression and although we may not prove definitively that the reason is stress, it is in fact implicit throughout this book. What we must do is discover what engenders the stress. Only when we understand totally what is causing the illness, do we have the opportunity of recovery. This is going to differ from person to person. It may not be easy to find, it may produce some discomfort, we may be surprised or even shocked at what we do find. However, until we uncover it for ourselves, beginning with a desire to do this, we shall simply stagger from day to day in a stupor, having no joy and little interest or effectiveness in our lives. We have to be ruthlessly objective and totally honest with ourselves. It must be done and it can be done.

Let's make a start. Generally speaking, we all have three main areas in our lives:

- Work or school or college or home
- Family
- Social or leisure

These are not in any particular priority (for me, my family is by far the most important part of my life), but probably the order in which stress is most likely to feature.

Work

It may be that you go out to work like most people do. You may not currently have a job because of redundancy, illness etc. You may be a housewife or mother at home; nonetheless a part of your day is work and it may well be a very high percentage of your day. You may be a student at school, college or university. Part of your time there is work, hopefully a fair portion of it. You may be in prison; some of your life is, or can be, labour. Whatever your situation, there is always some job to be done, paid or unpaid.

Why does work stress us? More importantly, why does it stress you personally or the person you are concerned about? This is subjective and ultimately only you can sort it out. I know why work oppressed me and I can speak for myself particularly and then propose some ideas generally.

I was and am dismayed, and sometimes angered, by the attitude (as I discerned it) of the 'management' towards the clients and staff in the system in which I was involved. You can read for 'system' – education, health, commerce, manufacturing, government*, etc. With certain exceptions the leadership emerges, in my perception, as both selfish and mediocre. They appear concerned only when looking out for themselves and have little, if any, respect or heed for anyone else. This is generally compounded by a display of pride and a belief that their policies are so wonderful that they should not even be questioned. After the programme has been enforced and operating for a while, there is a U-turn. We hear no apologies for the failure, just 'very good reasons' why there has to be yet another change of direction, which looks to be no better than the original fiasco. There is a proverb – "Where there is no vision, the people perish." *Book written before General Election 1st May 1997.*

You may conclude that the above is a somewhat feeble basis for stress, but after experiencing around 20 and more years of poor management, (during some 40 years of working life), there is undoubtedly a cumulative effect which eventually becomes overwhelming. Also, it seems to me that during these 40 years there has been a marked deterioration of standards, but may be each generation says that anyway about the previous one. When I began my apprenticeship, I thought managers cared more about standards and their charges, but perhaps I was just younger and more naive. Also, during and immediately after the war (I was born a year or so before the Second World War) there was a common bond between people joining together to survive and overcome the very real threat to any sort of democratic living.

Having committed this proposition to paper and read it through, I have to confess that it comes across as a rather simple and self-evident complaint. However, it took me a long time to discern that this was the reason for my work stress and hence depression. It may or may not be yours. I walked and pondered for many months before I realised my own trouble for myself, but now I know, and that knowledge brings understanding and relief. You may be quicker or slower than I was. Indeed, work might not pressure you at all, or it might be a totally different aspect of your employment, e.g. bullying, passed over for promotion, etc. Only you can discover what your own predicament is, but you can detect it. Right now, you may not be interested in finding out, or you may have done so but think there is nothing you can do about it, for instance, you may have lost a very good and unrepeatable job. You may have a vague idea but dare not investigate fully for fear of what you may find. Whatever your situation, there are solutions and we discuss these in later chapters.

Family

In the following chapter, we will consider a general concept which pertains to each of these three areas but for now we will reflect how family life can bring us tension as well as joy.

It may be that you have almost no family. I knew someone in this situation. There was a relative about 20 miles away who never communicated and one in America who did infrequently by letter. This was the sum total. There are those who have literally none known at all. This in itself may lead to depression. We all want to belong somewhere. Sometimes family has to be colleagues at work, in a home, in prison, wherever, because there are no blood relatives extant. Since we are all one family of the human race, this can presumably be tolerable but clearly not desirable.

When loved ones are ill, there is naturally stress. When they die the pain and trauma can be almost overwhelming. As my counsellor said to me, "Loss is always a component in depression." We expect to lose our grandparents and parents, nonetheless it hurts. We do not envisage losing a spouse until old age, but it happens. We expect our children to outlive us, but sometimes they do not. We can lose our children even while they are with us – babies grow into toddlers, infant school pupils, juniors, secondary youths, young men and women, men and women, fathers and mothers. They can stray from us because their behaviour is different from ours. They may shock or offend us.

Then there is unrighteous dominion, to employ a scriptural phrase. This is when we are forced to do things that we do not want to do (this is such an important concept that the following chapter is devoted to it). Those things may be good or bad. The enforcer, who may be a domineering spouse, parent, colleague, etc., may or may not have good intentions. There can be verbal and physical abuse. This can be an exceedingly complex subject because the effects can reach far into the future. Doubtless there is sufficiency of expert literature available in libraries and bookshops.

It is remarkable how much stress occurs within and between families. Christmas, I read, is one of the worst times. Rows and rifts appear as the pressures of different lifestyles collide in the festive season.

Social

There may sometimes be coercion even in our social lives but considerably less than the previous headings because we can generally choose our community activities. Customarily we have an acceptable selection of work, especially when younger and capable of changing job without too much difficulty, but usually our colleagues are selected without reference to us. We have no say in the matter of parents and brothers and sisters and other relatives. In the western world we decide on our spouse ourselves.

Socially, we should be safe but even here there can be trouble. After we join the club (golf, skating, bridge, tennis, drama, etc.), we encounter a family environment, which may well consist of a hierarchical structure. As time progresses, we may find that we like the activity but not the members, or that 80 per cent of pleasure is nullified by the 20 per cent of aggravation which is unavoidable. We may have to give up (loss) or we may become too old to participate (loss).

I would like to conclude this chapter with a few comments on a factor which affects us throughout our lives. This is not really an area as the previous three are, so I cannot label it number four. It is a part of us always. It is our health.

Currently we are in depression, or think that we might be or that someone we care about might be. This in itself is a grave illness but it may be that there are other health problems which have contributed to the depression. I met a young man who had been injured in a car accident in his mid-20s. His back was damaged, although you would never have realised as you watched his athletic skills. However, he was in permanent pain, sometimes bad, sometimes not so bad, but it was always with him. He had contemplated ending it all. Fortunately, he had not succumbed and now has no intention of doing so, but the thoughts had been accommodated temporarily. Similarly, as a tinnitus sufferer, fortuitously the roaring sound in his head gradually faded away to nothing.

As far as I am aware, nobody feels good when they are ill. You may love your family, your work and your leisure, but when you are on the sick list, your enjoyment is marred. The extent of the impairment is probably proportional to the degree of the illness; the worse you feel, lesser the joy you have.

Summary

It is imperative that we recognise and understand the cause(s) of our depression so that the correct remedial action may be implemented (recovery techniques are outlined later in the book). Generally, depression-forming stress originates from work, family or social activities or from health problems.

Chapter 4
The Underlying Origin of All Depression

You might deem the title of this chapter to be overconfident and presumptuous, but I am completely satisfied that there is just one fundamental source of all depression. When we understand it fully and apply it ourselves in our own unique and personal circumstances the problem will be laid bare, it will be out in the open. We shall still have to deal with it but it will be clearly visible. The enemy will have no cover left. It may be a Goliath, but he was a solitary figure and the right weapon in the right hands laid him flat and defenceless.

The problem is all to do with situation ownership. This is a simple sentence but the key to all stress and hence depression. Now that I can appreciate the incidents of the last few years of my own life, it is all patently obvious to me, but it required many hours of walking and pondering to arrive at this verdict. Can we begin the discussion with some straightforward examples and then progress to more subtle illustrations?

Two pursuits which I practise are racing dinghy sailing and ice-skating. As you may be aware, dinghies are small boats with generally too much sail area. This is to create speed at the expense of comfort. Sailing fast on a broad reach in a strong wind in an estuary set among the beautiful mountains of North Wales is altogether exhilarating. The hull planes across the surface, bounces against the tops of waves, there is wind in your face and spray everywhere and you shout for joy. Moments later you are struck by a twisting squall which turns the boat on its side with the sail disappearing beneath the surface and you are floundering in the water. A cloud covers the sun. The sea is cold and grey and the nearest bank is half a mile away. There is no other craft about. The rip tide is carrying you towards the mouth of the estuary and the open sea beyond. In a few seconds you have lurched from complete and pleasurable control of events to virtually none at all. The ownership of the situation has transposed dramatically. You now have no choice but to struggle hard to bring the boat upright to restore the earlier conditions.

You might be skating on a normal session at the ice rink. The music is playing, you can hear the edges of your blades cutting into the ice as you swerve round the rink dodging past the other skaters. You feel really great. During a moment's inattention you trip in a groove. You reach out with your hands to save yourself and break a wrist as you hit the hard surface. You are still moving fast while you sprawl helplessly on the ice. You are unable to regain your feet because your wrist hurts and you are in shock. You crash into the barrier and dislocate your shoulder. You have been reduced from great delight to a long wait in the hospital casualty queue. Ownership of the situation has passed entirely from you.

You are driving through the night along the motorway with the rain pelting down. Your favourite music tape is playing softly because your family is all asleep. You are enroute for the ferry and a great summer holiday (the continental weather forecast is good). Suddenly there is a dreadful noise under the floor as the gearbox grinds itself to pieces. You did not pay the additional premium for the extra holiday insurance because the car has just been serviced. Unfortunately, your breakdown membership has lapsed. You were in control, but not anymore.

You had a good job and then redundancy appears from nowhere. "Here is your severance pay, clear your bench and locker and be out of the building in ten minutes." You are happily married until your spouse leaves a note to say it is all over. You think that your health is sound and then the X-ray plate contains an ominous patch. In each context you imagined you were all right and then you were not. It was not necessarily your fault, it just happened.

These examples are dramatic and loss of possession of the circumstances is clearly demonstrated. The boating, skating and driving are cases where there will be no prolonged adverse effects (as long as your wrist mends properly). They caused temporary stress at the time but once the difficulties were overcome, it disappeared, and you can look back and laugh about it. We all experience this type of setback; it is a part of life.

However, loss of employment, spouse or health over a sustained period of time may well result in depression unless the loss is made good. We can probably all handle stress for a short while but what if it is every day, every week, every month, every year? That which is shrugged off in a couple of weeks can become a major burden when repeated daily with no end in sight. If a bath tap drips for long enough, it wears off the surface to generate a permanent scar. In my own experience I could apparently handle what I perceived to be bad management in small doses but when it became a persistent feature over the years it became unbearable, and I was wholly ignorant of the pressure that was building up.

A prime example must be prisoners. I would imagine that most of them suffer from depression due to stress. They might know the term of incarceration, they might not. It might be months, years, or even life. There might be abuse from fellow inmates and warders or guards. Undoubtedly there is physical deterioration. It must be horribly degrading to have your lifestyle and possibly even your life at the whim of another. There must be fear, distress, anger, despair and most, if not all, of the negative emotions we undergo. A prisoner, on the surface at any rate, does not control the situation but even here we shall find that there is opportunity to exercise free agency. As we briefly examine the areas of the previous chapter, we shall find that we are all, at first glance, prisoners to a certain extent in that our freedom appears curtailed to a greater or lesser degree.

Let's start with work again. The odds are that you have a boss, and he has a boss, and so on. He (or she) may be a good manager in that he cares for his staff, resources, clients etc.; he may not. If you and he are at loggerheads and he has the final say, then you do not own the situation. His decisions may be wrong absolutely, they may be wrong relatively or subjectively. If you have to work with a 'bad' boss, then over the months and years you will be under strain.

You may be the employer. Your staff may stress you and there may be additional demands – obtaining orders, selling products, moving premises, cash flow problems, etc. You might be a teacher with unruly pupils and mounds of irrelevant administrative chores. You might be a nurse or doctor with too much paperwork and too little time for your patients.

You may have a 'good' boss and a lousy job. You have no inclination to open letters all day, but you need the money and the pay is reasonable. If there is compulsion, the control is not yours.

Whether you are forced by people or circumstances, it makes no difference. If you have to do it, you are not in charge.

These comments about employment apply in a similar way to family. When we bring children into the world we are obliged to look after them. For most parents this is a joy. It certainly is for me especially when they were little. The relationships evolve as they grow up but it is still a wonderful thing. However, there are family relationships where there is abuse towards spouse, children, parents and so on. This is shameful, and results in terrible stress. You do not own the situation when you are trapped in dreadful family conditions and cannot see a way out.

If there are upsets due to social or leisure activities we can apply choice and do something else. This may give us the occasional sleepless night but hopefully we can sort it out.

Poor health can overshadow every waking hour. We have some jurisdiction over our own health, but by no means, total. Generally, our afflictions just arrive.

Summary

If we are rarely able to be proactive (making our own decisions) and spend most of our time in conditions where we have to react to external events, the ensuing stress will eventually cause depression. This can occur at work, in the family environment, when socialising and through poor health. There may be a massive trauma (almost certainly resulting from loss) which is unresolved. There may be minor complaints which wear us down as the years pass by. However, we shall find that there is hope and an answer, whatever our conditions.

Chapter 5
The History of a Particular
Personal Depression

I have found that I need an account of what was and is happening to me, and I keep a daily record. At the moment I am recovering and I think that the first sign of a steady improvement was when my documentation began. There was no record before diagnosis because I was not aware that I was sick. However, I have maintained a journal for many years although the entries have not been on a daily basis by any means.

I shall summarise relevant features from my one hundred and more A4 handwritten sheets. They are all important to me but only a precis will be of use to you. Your own record, when you start it (if you do not have one already) will be valuable to you in every detail. It is of no consequence when these events took place, as to the actual date, but chronology is necessary, so there is a time axis of years passed on the charts. As an engineer, if I am constructing equipment, I require a circuit to study, design, test and modify. Similarly, with my health, I find that a 'picture' of events is vital if I am to understand what happened to me before and after diagnosis of depression. Necessarily, the experiences before are recalled retrospectively and depend on memory and notes. Therefore, they are not as precise as those registered in detail during recuperation.

Chart 1 shows a period of about thirteen years with some event markers. As you can see, there is nothing spectacular, but these commonplace occurrences are significant in the development of my illness. They conveyed nothing to me at the time but from my present position I now realise that they were signposts with depression written all over them. Hopefully, you will recognise your own indicators in your own life. I am certain that if you spot them early enough you will be able to avoid a considerable amount of suffering.

On **Chart 1** there is a span of some four years between definitely no depression and definitely depression. I cannot recollect it any more accurately than that, so I have taken the midpoint quite arbitrarily as the commencement of the illness. It was diagnosed some six years later, which is a long time.

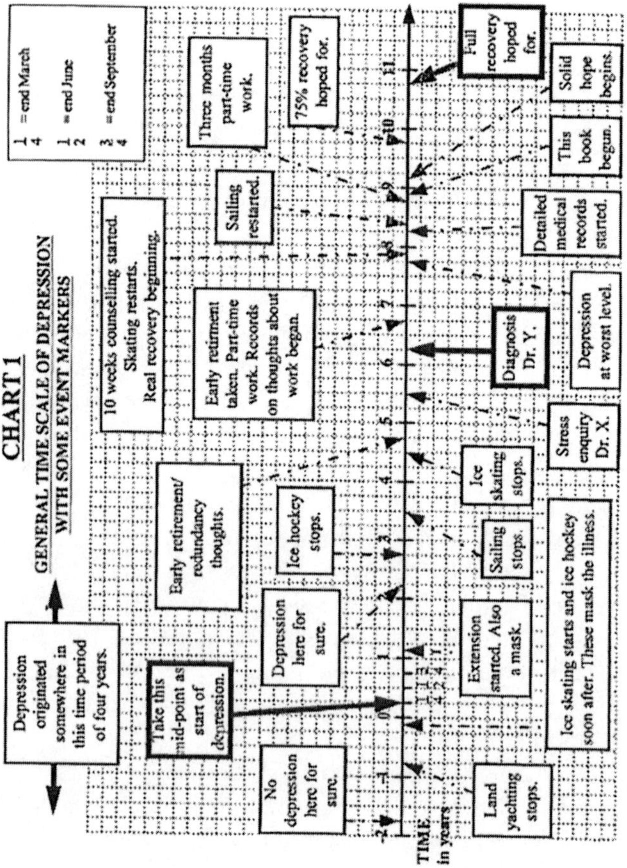

CHART 1

GENERAL TIME SCALE OF DEPRESSION WITH SOME EVENT MARKERS

I remember the appointment clearly. It was with a doctor whom I had not seen before (Dr Y on the chart). It was to be my 'lucky' day. I had jotted down three items needing attention – sore throat for several days, did I require antibiotics? – what had happened to the hospital referral for the removal of polyps from my nose? – and could I quickly discuss stress? She asked me for the symptoms (which I had previously drafted), and I listed them. When I had finished, she informed me that it sounded like depression. Even as she spoke, I knew she was right and I started crying. There was both shock and relief. I was in shock to know that I was so ill, and relieved that there was a reason why I felt so bad. There have been many occasions when nobody else has taken any notice other than lip service. This doctor saved my sanity and probably my life.

She said initially that it was mild depression. I think this was so that I would not be unduly alarmed. The 'mild' was increased to 'significant' soon afterwards. In fact, it was deep-rooted, serious and life-threatening. Six years (and it may have been more, probably nearer eight) of severe depression is a considerable load to carry.

The previous tentative mention of discussion of stress to another practitioner (Dr X on the chart), who brushed it aside, had been a year or so earlier. I would surmise that the last year before diagnosis accounted for a substantial proportion of the illness. I must have been very sick to have even broached the subject the first time and there was still a year of ignorant suffering to go. Also, I am sure the depression versus time graph is a curve which becomes increasingly steep, an acceleration rather than a velocity.

Furthermore, there is an element of overshoot, because the lowest point on the chart is around one-and-a-half years after diagnosis, and solid recovery underway some months after that. Thus, identification transpired six years after the assumed start of depression, the lowest period after seven-and-a-half years, and recovery underway after eight years or so. Hopefully, recovery will be well advanced within a year of its commencement and complete within another year or so.

It will be productive to examine the events charted in more detail. In the final chapters, there are guidelines for you to help yourself (or someone else) and you will need to construct your own chart. My warning signs were not significant at the time but looking back it is clear that depression was on the way.

With reference to my sporadic journal, photographs, cine film, etc., I could confidently register the no depression and depression markers. They are both at Easter time. For many years, we have taken family holidays at the seaside, during the school half-tens in spring and again in autumn, and so we have records of them. Even so, I can only be sure of the two of them, and as recounted earlier, in order to have a starting point, I placed it in the middle.

Two events occurred prior to this which are both important. The first is land yachting stops. Because we took our half-term holidays out of season there are very few people about. Where we stayed there is a firm sandy beach some two miles long, windswept and deserted. I managed to procure a second hand land yacht, which is basically a low-slung frame with three wheels and a sail. It travels at 40mph in a good wind and even faster in a gale. It can be sailed in reasonable conditions as family fun and as a solo machine in rough weather when it is extremely exhilarating. We had a lot of fun with it for several years and then the time came when I just could not be bothered to trail it to the beach, rig it, sail it, pull it up the stones, and derig it, especially in the wind and rain with freezing fingers.

You could say I don't blame you, we all stop activities at some stage, you can't go on forever, etc. I was not particularly dismayed that it was over, it was all too much of a fuss. If someone had placed it fully rigged on the sand and was prepared to deal with it afterwards, then, on a nice day, I would probably have had a go. I did not think, *Ah yes, this is depression starting,* but looking back, that is what it was.

The second feature was the inception of ice skating and ice hockey. The church youth decided to try out the newly opened ice rink as one of their Friday night activities. Since my daughter was only ten years old, I joined them to look after her. We hired those dreadfully uncomfortable blunt skates and holding well-gloved hands for mutual support, we staggered round. As a young man had been a reasonably proficient skater, but that night, a quarter of a century later, I was useless. At the end I sat down with aching legs and pinched feet, grateful that it was a one-off visit, but my daughter loved it. "Can we come again, Dad?" I pointed out all the difficulties but to no avail. We located a combined session for both children and parents and a weekly activity was initiated.

Once it was inevitable, I resolved to try to skate properly again. Our other children elected to come and brought friends as well. Most of us purchased our own boots and I found my old love of skating returning. I began to go by myself during the lunchtime session and whenever I had a half-day, and I attained the competence of my younger days.

My job was such that if you worked an evening, you were given a half-day off in lieu of pay. One year my schedule allowed me to be free on Monday afternoons. When I arrived at the ice rink, I was informed that Monday afternoons would now be ice hockey practice. That day, however, you could skate on one half of the ice or join the hockey people in the other half. In future, there would be all hockey and no public skating.

They lent me a hockey stick and we skated round pushing the puck. I was instantly enthralled, I thought it was brilliant. The coach was a genial Canadian fresh from the National Hockey League across the Atlantic and he really knew the game. He taught us, beginners and experienced, from scratch. He showed us how to skate and how to hit the puck. He was superb. I had a fantastic session. I was totally captivated. Like a little boy, I looked forward to my Monday practice. I bought my own kit and attended regular training in the evening as well, and eventually played in matches. For me, it was the greatest game that I had ever played.

Unfortunately, the hockey masked my illness. I was completely ignorant of my depression and this wonderful new interest in life simply buried it even deeper. This meant that it remained unrecognised but was still generating damage. The causes of stress and hence depression persisted unchanged. The ailment festered on in secret. Depression can only be cured when the underlying problems are fully understood so that appropriate remedies can be applied.

A further masking occurred when I began building an extension to the back of the house. We were finding that there was just not enough room downstairs. I obtained a number of quotations which were much costlier than expected, so I decided to have a go myself. This was a completely new experience for me, as was the hockey, and initially I found them both absorbing, but the unfortunate side effect was that they disguised the depression.

Some two-and-a-half years later after skating and hockey began, I can say for certain that I was suffering from depression. I am aware of that now. At the time I had no idea. About six months after this, the ice hockey stopped. It was simply too much trouble. The training took place on Mondays at midnight (ice time was very scarce) and sometimes we were still banging the puck around at three or even four o'clock in the morning. One guy was a baker, he went straight to work, no sleep at all. You did not feel tired while you were playing because the excitement and adrenalin kept you on a high, but Tuesday after lunch it hit you really hard. This became too much hassle and I packed it up by degrees and finally altogether.

The following summer, I could not be bothered with the nuisance of launching and retrieving the dinghies, so the sailing was stopped. The summer after that was the end of the skating, the extension was thankfully finished by now and that autumn I found myself with serious thoughts about finishing work. I did my projected financial calculations, pension etc., income versus future expenditure, and considered various termination dates and how I might employ myself afterwards. These thoughts remained with me and I did a lot of walking and pondering on my own. I still had no intimation that I was in deep depression.

The next summer, when I was attending the Health Centre for some minor complaint which I thought required anti-biotics, I tentatively asked the doctor about stress. The reply, as I recall, was that we all have stress and we have to live with it (I emphasise that this was not my beautiful, life-saving doctor). The following Easter, my doctor (the beautiful, life-saving one) diagnosed depression. It was finally out in the open after six years, may be more.

I would like to return to Chart 1 again in a later chapter when we are reviewing recovery.

Summary

There were clear pointers to depression which were not recognised at the time. As with the symptoms of Chapter 1, any one of them itself might not be significant, but taken together it becomes obvious – land yachting stops, hockey stops, sailing stops, skating stops, work becomes a chore (generally I have enjoyed it), I ask a doctor about stress. The skating, hockey and extension cloaked the illness and delayed the diagnosis.

In Chapters 9, 10 and 12 there are recommendations for recognising your own warning signs.

Chapter 6
The Inevitability of a Religious Aspect

I put 'inevitable' because, as far as I know, when people find themselves in distress, they eventually turn to their god. I believe that Christians appreciate Psalm 23 – "Yeah, though I walk through the valley of the shadow of death, I will fear no evil: for thou art with me". Presumably other religions have their own favourite, comforting writings. People tend to start or restart prayer and supplicate their maker for relief.

Obviously, I have no knowledge of the state of your religious or atheistic beliefs or activity, but thoroughly recommend that you read this chapter with at least as much consideration as any of the others. You will find that it is important in the understanding of depression whatever your own personal views in these matters. I suppose that our opinions are as private or public as anything else, for example marital status, political orientation, etc., and so I would prefer to comment in fairly general terms while relating those of my individual experiences which are not totally personal to me.

Some 20 years before the determined starting date of my depression, I was in trouble. Although I was happy with my marriage, my work, my health, our holidays, possessions, leisure activities, etc., I had no inkling as to what I was doing here. I was totally ignorant of the purpose, if any, of my existence. I had no grasp of how I had arrived where I was, and even less idea where I was going. If my current lifestyle had continued until death, I felt it was undoubtedly an exercise in futility. I had no function in life. I wanted the truth.

I studied different types of literature: philosophical, religious (western and eastern), humanitarian, Darwin's "Origin of Species", etc., which helped not one whit. I had no idea what the truth was that I sought, but I did know that I had not located it. The search lasted five years or so. During this period, I became greatly and then totally preoccupied with finding the absolute reason for my being on this earth. Eventually I arrived at the Bible with particular reference to the four gospels of the New Testament.

I became convinced that the answer, whatever it might be, lay somewhere in these four books – Matthew, Mark, Luke and John; and I read them through in that sequence. My understanding was only superficial but I believed in the words and deeds of the Saviour, Jesus Christ. I accepted all his teachings and all his miracles. There was nothing rational about this, it was just a feeling, but it was overpowering and filled my soul with an absolute, unshakeable certainty.

I could not read about his death, it was too much for me, so as soon as he was captured by the guards after his betrayal, I advanced through the narrative to the resurrection. On Wednesday evenings I attended a Bible study class at the local church. They were unable to answer my questions but were most tolerant and friendly. This was just as well because I informed the minister that I did not believe that his organisation was in possession of the truth and that if I ever unearthed it, then I would let him know. However, I was unable to do this because when I finally arrived at absolute reality, he had departed to pastures new. I doubt if he would have believed me anyway.

We moved house to the other side of the city and only weeks later two young men knocked on our front door, announced that they were missionaries and asked if I read the Bible. I answered affirmatively but only the four gospels. They then inquired whether I would be prepared to discuss these with them. I agreed to this and they, and others came around, some one hundred times over the next few months. They expounded some amazing concepts, many of which appeared to me to be quite preposterous. Not the least among their assertions was that the church to which they belonged was the only one recognised by the Saviour and the only one with pure doctrine, which was received by revelation from the Saviour himself. Despite their far-fetched ideas, I continued to listen and question and discuss. During my earlier investigations of other philosophies, I had little difficulty in dismissing them as simply man-made ideas, but this was so different and yet so appealing. I could not leave it alone.

My purpose is not to preach but to explain how my religious knowledge affected my response to my illness. Suffice to say that on a particular day and time that I will never forget, the heavens opened to me personally, and I received individual revelation that what they were teaching me was correct. As you can imagine, I was totally stunned. At last my searching was over. It had taken such a long time, but when the answer came, it was unmistakable. What I knew that day, I know today, and always will.

I would like to elaborate on the Plan of Salvation as expounded in the Bible and other scriptures. Again, the intent is not to evangelise per se, but to gain an understanding of what is happening to us. This assists in all aspects of life. Indeed, it is essential to know the end of our existence if we are to have ownership of the situation. However, if you are satisfied with your present situation, you will not appreciate that it is requisite, but since you are reading this, the chances are that you are in some kind of trouble, and so you will find that a global picture will be of great assistance to you. It helped me then and still does now, although I would underline that at the time I did not have depression or any other serious illness. I was just ignorant, which to me is not bliss, it is abhorrent.

The basic truth can be outlined with a simple diagram and a couple of paragraphs.

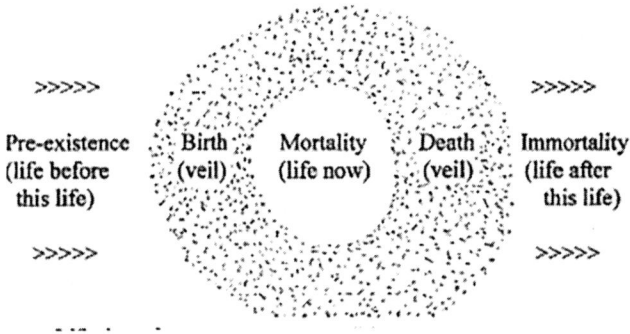

| Pre-existence (life before this life) | Birth (veil) | Mortality (life now) | Death (veil) | Immortality (life after this life) |

Life has three estates or conditions. In the first, the pre-existence, we looked much as we do now but we were in spirit form. Our bodies were spirit only, with shape but no solid substance. We had intelligence as at present and could communicate and make decisions. At birth (or just before) the spirit passes through the veil of forgetfulness and enters the body to begin earth life as a little baby having no recollection of the premortal existence. (This is nothing to do with the false notion of reincarnation). We are the same people in a different state. We live our lives in mortality where we are now, and sooner or later we die, at which point our spirit lives on and returns through the veil to the pre-existence leaving the body behind. This life, however short or long, is a vital stage in our overall progression.

Eventually there will be a resurrection and everyone will regain their physical frames. These bodies of flesh and bone will then be perfect and indestructible. We shall all have perfect heath with no illness and we shall live forever. This takes place for everybody and is termed immortality. However, the quality of life during immortality depends on how we have behaved while on this earth in conformity with the knowledge and the desires of our hearts which we had during this life. This is why mortality is so very important, particularly for those of us who attain the age of accountability (little children are not answerable for anything). There will be a judgement to determine our various destinations so that the righteous, who will still be righteous, do not have to dwell with the wicked, who will still be wicked. This judgement will be totally equitable. Those who were honourable will receive their worthy reward, those who were evil will receive their due, and those in between will receive theirs as appropriate. There is a God, he is just, and will exercise judgement. This is absolute truth, independent of any beliefs, no matter how sincerely they may be held. As you can imagine, there is a lot more to this than has been presented here, and you are most welcome to more details if you want them. The object of this chapter is to introduce the basic picture of complete reality, which was a necessity in my life and which, in fact, is a necessity for everybody, although you may well have other ideas.

At this juncture I would like to repeat the fruitlessness of suicide. Sometimes depression is so acute that the sufferer concludes that the only solution is to end his life. In my view, he is then so ill that he does not really know what he is doing. Presumably he thinks that this will resolve all his problems, but in actuality he will only exchange the current ones for another set – some different, some similar – because death is not terminal in the eternal perspective, it is only a physical transposition. Our personalities are unaltered when we die, we just relinquish our bodies. We still think and feel as we do now with the same hopes, aspirations, fears and worries as at present. We do not black out; we progress to a diverse domain – the same spirit world that we left behind to come here. The chances are that we would feel disappointed if we deliberately took an early bath from the football field. If we were to leave the game without telling anybody, we would most likely regret it later, and, of course, the remaining players would have to struggle on by themselves. If we were to curtail our mortal existence ourselves, we would leave our families grieving, and looking back we might well rue it.

Summary

People who are ill or in distress often turn to God. It is vital that we have access to the truth concerning our existence so that we may have a solid basis for situation ownership and hence improvement in health. To be part of a system which is ultimately fair and just (even though present conditions are by no means always so) gives us a sense of safety and security. Once we have an overall picture with an eternal perspective, we can work out our own destiny, which gives us control of our lives, not only here and now, but forever. This management will enable us to track down the right solutions for our own particular problems.

Chapter 7
The Road to Recovery
Part 1 – The Production of Written Records

Could I ask you to re-examine **Chart 1,** where, you may remember, we had reached the diagnosis at Easter after 6 years of illness? The next marker is in the following September, when I took early retirement. This came about in a fortuitous way (if you believe in luck and coincidence, which I do not). Only days after my doctor pronounced depression, a memo, which was masterfully vague, arrived on my desk. It hinted that there might possibly be the opportunity for early release and anyone who might be interested could so indicate. I had always said that if my work ever started to make me ill, then I would leave, regardless of any consequences. There is no doubt that the health of the breadwinner is of primary importance, not only for future income generation, but even more urgently for attending to parental duties. I instantly applied. I had done my financial calculations and my pondering some eighteen months previously and no further cogitation was needed. When it was offered, I accepted in writing the very next day. This speed of response surprised the management, but they did not know that my deliberations had been underway for eighteen months.

In September I worked on a part-time basis at a couple of organisations and began documenting how to generate income during retirement, because I deemed that I was still young enough to continue making some sort of contribution to society. Written records are for me, and probably for you, essential. This paperwork also contained thoughts and feelings concerning my health. Initially everything went pretty well and, indeed, I applied for two full-time positions, which was totally unrealistic at my age, but indicative of a good level of general health.

At this stage I would like to draw your attention to **Chart 2,** which is an expanded form of **Chart 1** from *diagnosis Dr Y* onwards. You will notice that the horizontal axis is an enlarged time scale of **Chart 1.** The vertical axis is numbered from 0 to 100, which I will now explain.

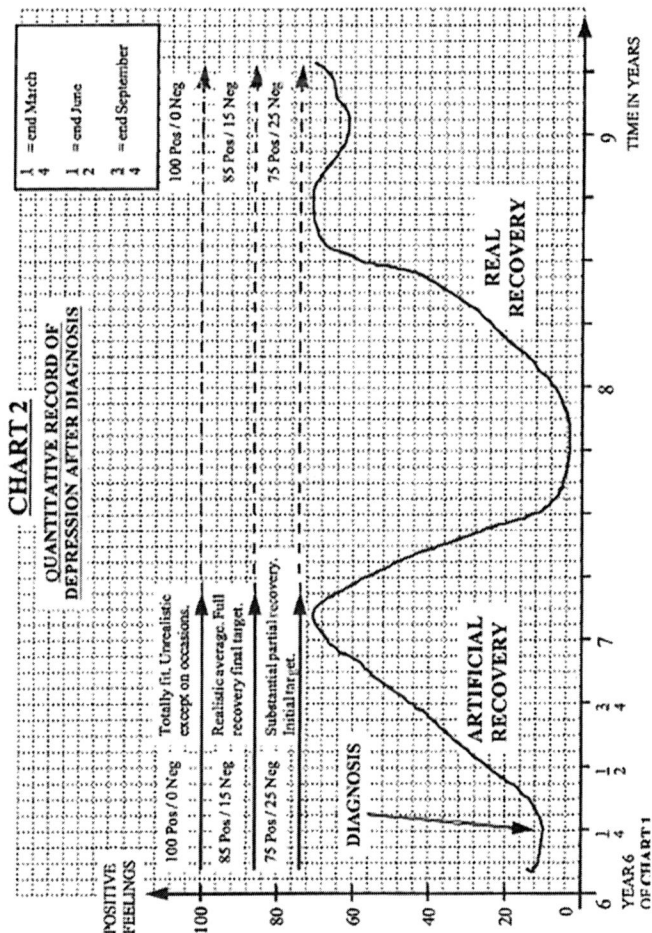

CHART 2

QUANTITATIVE RECORD OF
DEPRESSION AFTER DIAGNOSIS

Some two years after diagnosis I decided to map out my progress. As an engineer, the only satisfactory method for me is a graph. In order to plot this, you require numbers, that is to say, you need to quantify how you feel. This is, of course, highly subjective and can only be an approximation. Nonetheless, as long as the measuring technique is sensibly constant, a trend can be established so that we can observe whether there is improvement or deterioration.

My marking scheme comprises numbers positive/negative. At the one extreme is 100/0, which is 100 positive/0 negative, when I feel absolutely brilliant. This could happen when I am out sailing on a beautiful summer day. Conversely 0/100 is 0 positive/1 00 negative, when I am in total depression. Neither extreme occurs frequently. *50/50* means my feelings are overall neutral – some of the time they were good, and some of the time they were bad. The smallest measurement sub-division is 5, for example 65/35, although averaging calculations can produce decimals which are rounded to the nearest 1. Only the positive figure is plotted on the graph but I find that keeping the negative figure in mind assists with the initial estimate. We are attempting to quantify the unquantifiable as we assign numbers to feelings but it is, for me anyway, the only technique to observe progress.

I then needed a time period over which this monitoring would be effected. Since emotions can swing quite violently during the day, the interval should be less than a full day and I settled on three:

AM – morning, from waking to lunchtime

PM – from lunchtime to teatime

Eve – from teatime to sleeping at bedtime.

I completed the day's figures (and any comments) just prior to going to bed and if I had second thoughts between then and sleeping, the *eve* number would be adjusted the following day. I also made a note of work – decorating, housework, gardening, paying bills in town, mending appliances, reading the jobs adverts, etc., (I was off real work at the time); when I slept during the day; and there was also a column for remarks. At the end of the week I did averaging calculations and after six weeks the overall value was plotted on the graph.

Three consecutive weeks are shown as: **Table 1** – Mon 8/5 to Sun 14/5 **Table** 2 – Mon 15/5 to Sun 21/5 **Table** 3 – Mon *2215* to Sun 28/5

They are abstracted from my health diary charts of the month of May of Year 8 of **Chart 1.** It is worth considering these briefly before returning to **Chart 2.**

Table 1 indicates a bad few days. Even the two skating sessions were poor at 20/80 and 10/90, the walk with one of my children was only 20/80, the visit Thurs eve 30/70, and even with all the family together merely 40/60, which was the top mark. There was nothing especially unusual to cause these poor marks. I was not particularly discouraged. When you have a miserable week, you just plod on and may be the next will pick up. Doubtless there is a reason why we have our ups and downs – chemistry, diet, emotion, dreams, fatigue, suppressed thoughts, weather, etc., but sometimes it is unfathomable. You try to enjoy the good, and keep going during the troubles.

Table 2 is much more encouraging. The depression feelings have improved from 19 to 57 (positive), an increase of some 200%; the daytime sleeps have dropped from 6 to 5, a decrease of around 17%; the work hours have grown by about 8% from 1.3 to 1.4 hours per day. Why should this be? Again, there is little that is unfamiliar. Perhaps the weather was very sunny. The Saturday comment is interesting – "Bad at times. Pressure means loss of control of the day". I have no recollection of that day or even that week, but I have to conclude that the first five days were more or less mine (resulting in very tolerable scores) and then, on Saturday afternoon and evening circumstances must have been beyond my control. I hate weddings and most formal functions which I was obliged to attend, and my walk was delayed. I then 'messed about', suggesting that I was still at the wedding, and my sleep was also postponed. Nonetheless, if every week was that favourable, I would not complain at all.

Table 3 is most illuminating. I selected it deliberately and then took the two previous ones without bothering what they contained. This third table is not at all representative of an average week but it surely demonstrates the immense power of motivation.

Some four years earlier I had bought another Fireball sailing dinghy (a very fast trapeze racing craft) because my current one had expired of old age. The 'new' one had remained covered up in my front garden from the day of purchase. I fetched it from Essex, the owner was buying something else, put the cover on when I arrived home and it stood unmoved over the years until, on week beginning May 22nd, I had the urge to use it on our forthcoming Spring bank holiday. My enthusiasm once I got started was commensurate with when I first held an ice- hockey stick. The trailer, trolley, boat and rigging all required attention. As you can see from **Table** 3, it took me the whole week, on and off. It is worth examining each entry.

Monday – clearly a good skating session which set me up in the right frame of mind; town and Fireball preparation went well; and then more work on the boat after a family meeting. The first two periods scored very high at 90/1 0, and the evening tailed off slightly with tiredness to 80/20. No sleep, I was too engrossed. Total 260. Excellent day, sunny throughout, as I recall. I was interested in what I was doing and I was outside in the sun most of the time.

Tuesday – the marks are only marginally less at 240. Most of the day devoted to the Fireball. Only 2 hours work recorded, so I clearly did not count this as work, which would have been 'town, shop, taxi children'. Slight loss of situation ownership here, but still a very good day. No sleep again, most unusual.

Wednesday – two periods of boat preparation, a mere half-hour sleep (in three days), followed by 'meetings', which pulled the day average to a still very respectable 210.

Thursday – best day of the week with 270 points – exceptional. The day was all mine, I suited myself (apart from the inevitable providing sandwiches, meals, washing-up, etc.)

– good skating and fireball preparation (I wonder what the two hours work was?) No sleep.

Friday – 230 points. A half-hour sleep needed. Some loss of control of circumstances in the evening. Also fatigue perhaps setting in as the boat now ready, and probably beginning to worry about the long haul to Wales the following day (only 165 miles, but sufficient to unsettle me because of the depression).

Saturday – late setting off on holiday, sleep obligatory half way, but, even so, 190 points.

Sunday – good day with a score of 240, no sleep as intent on sailing. Not recorded here, but I remember crashing out at bedtime and sleeping deeply for about twelve hours.

This was a very good week (I think it was sunny most of the time, which always helps), with an average of 78/22, bringing the three weeks mean to 51/49. We see from **Chart 2** that the graph was mid-50s and still climbing, though at a lesser rate, towards the end of May. (The six weeks figure, when plotted, would have been different from that of these 3 weeks. In fact, the graph shows 56/44 for the end of the month).

Summary

We have considered some particular methods of producing records so that we can follow the course of the depression in a quantitative way. Tables and charts have been constructed. These are my personal ideas. You may care to use them; you may decide to 'do your own thing'.

Table 1: Monday 8 to Sunday 14 May of Year 8

Day and Date	a.m.	p.m.	eve.	Comment	Work hours
MON 8 May	Walk. Read newspaper. Jono 30/70	Fill up forms. (Sleep) 30/70	Family discussion. 40/60	Not a very good day.	1
TUE 9 May	Ice skating. 20/80	Shopping. Town. Met friend 30/70	Fixed appliance. Read newspaper. Telephone hols. 30/70	Quite bad depression.	1/2
WED 10 May	Walk. Buy wood. 20/80	Decorate. 20/80	Meetings. 10/90	Bad day when decorating.	2

THU 11 May	(Sleep) Skate. 10/90	(Sleep) Shop. 20/80	Visit with one child. 30/70	Bad day	N/A
FRI 12 May	Walk. Decorate. 10/90	(Sleep) Housework. 10/90	YouTube meeting. 10/90	Bad day	
SAT 13 May	Shop. Walk. 10/90	(Sleep) Car repair. 10/90	Visit Cheltenham. 20/80	Bad day	N/A
SUN 14 May	Church. 10/90	(Sleep) Visitors. 10/90	Walk with one child. 20/80	Bad day	N/A

Add up the P numbers – Monday is 30 + 30 + 40 = 100, Tuesday is 80, Wednesday is 50, Thursday is 60, Friday is 30, Saturday is 40, Sunday is 40.

This gives a total of 100 + 80 + 50 + 60 + 30 + 40 + 40 = 400.

There are 3 sessions per day or 7 x 3 = 21 per week.

Average for this week = $\frac{400 \text{ Positive}}{21 \text{ Sessions}}$ = 19 P or 19P/81N.

Total number of day sleeps = 6. This is 6/7 for the week.

Total number of *work* hours (only during week days) = 3.5 which is $\frac{3.5 \text{ hours}}{5 \text{ days}}$ = 0.7 hours per day.

Summary – Depression feelings 19 Positive/81 Negative.
Daytime sleeping 6 out of 7.
Work 0.7 hours per day.

Overall – a bad week.

Table 2: Monday 15 to Sunday 21 May of Year 8

Day & Date	a.m.	p.m.	eve.	Comment	Work hours
MON 15 May	Skate. 30/70	DIY store. Met friend. (Sleep) Take car. 40/60	"Taxi children." 50/50	Improvement.	1½
TUE 16 May	Walk. Town. 60/40	Shopping. Paperwork. 80/20	Read paper. Watch TV. 70/30	Further improvement.	½
WED 17 May	Walk (v. wet). Fix cabinet. 80/20	Tidy up. Housework. 80/20	Meetings. 50/50	Feel OK about work September.	2
THU 18 May	Skate. 70/30	DIY store. Tidy up. (Sleep) 50/50	Visit with friend. 50/50	Average day.	1
FRI 19 May	Walk. Decorate. 70/30	Decorate. (Sleep). 80/20	Visit Cheltenham. 50/50	Still OK about work September.	2
SAT 20 May	Visit OAPs. Shop. 40/60	Wedding. Walk 40/60	Mess about. (Sleep) 50/50	Bed at times. Pressure means loss of control of day.	N/A
SUN 21 May	Church. 50/50	(Sleep) Walk. 60/40	Walk. Phone friend. 50/50	Average day.	N/A

Add up the P numbers = 1200 and divide by 21 sessions gives 1200/21 = 57 P or 57/43.

Total number of day sleeps = 5/7.

Total number of work hours = 7 over 5 days = 7/5 = 1.4 hours per day.

Summary for this week:

> Depression feelings 57 Positive/43Negative.
> Daytime sleeping 5 days out of 7.
> Work 1.4 hours per day.

Overall – a much better week.

Summary for the two weeks – The averaging process continues for six weeks before plotting the point on the graph. We have two weeks here.

Total P numbers = 400 last week + 1200 this week = 1600.

Total sessions = 2 x 21.
Average for the two weeks = $\frac{1600}{2 \times 21}$ = 38P/62N.

Total day sleep = 6 last week + 5 this week = 11 days out of 14.

Work hours = 6.5 + 7 = 13.5 out of 10 days
$= \frac{13.5 \text{ hours}}{10 \text{ days}}$ = 1.35 hours per day

Table 3: Monday 22 to Sunday 28 May of Year 8

Day and Date	a.m.	p.m.	eve.	Comment	Work hours
MON 22 May	Skating. 90/10	Town. Fireball preparation. 90/10	Finances. Family discussion. Fireball prep. 80/20	Motivation for Fireball prep. overcame tiredness.	2
TUE 23 May	Walk. Fireball prep. 80120	Town. Shopping. Fireball prep. 80/20	Fireball prep. Taxi children. 80/20	As above.	2
WED 24 May	Walk. Fireball prep. 80/20	Fireball prep. Accounts (Sleep) 80/20	Meetings. 50/50	As above.	2
THU 25 May	Skating. 90/10	Fireball prep. 90/10	Fireball prep. 90/10	As above.	2

FRI 26 May	Walk. Fireball prep. 90/10	Fireball prep. Shop. (Sleep) 80/20	Youth meeting. 60/40	As above.	2
SAT 27 May	Fireball on trailer. Shop. 70/30	Visit OAPs. Drive to Wales. (Sleep) 60/40	Drive to Wales. 60/40	Driving stress. Tired	*N/A*
SUN 28 May	Walk. Get Fireball ready. 80/20	Sailing Fireball in estuary. 80/20	Sailing Fireball In estuary. 80/20	Good day but tired.	*N/A*

Add up the P numbers = 1640 and divide by 21 sessions gives 1640/21 = 78 **P** or 78/22.

Total number of day sleeps = *317.*

Total number of *work* hours = 10 over 10 days = 10/5 = 2 hours per week.

Summary for this week:

> Depression feelings 78 Positive/22 Negative.
> Day-time sleeping 3 days out of 7.
> *Work* 2 hours per day.

Overall – an even better week again.

Summary for the three weeks – Continuing the averaging process:

Total P numbers = 400 + 1200 + 1640 = 3240.

Total sessions = 3 x 21.

Average for the three weeks = $\frac{3240}{3 \times 21}$ = 51P/49N.

Total day sleeps = 6 + 5 + 3 = 14 days out of 21.

Work hours 6.5 + 7 + 10 = 23.5 out of 15 days
$$= \frac{23.5}{15} = 1.57 \text{ hours per day.}$$

Chapter 8
The Road to Recovery
Part 2 – The Use of Written Records

In the previous chapter there was an introduction to the use of the documentation in that we analysed Table 3 in some detail to explain (retrospectively) why the feelings fluctuated. I would like to follow up with a closer survey of Chart 2.

After six years (at the minimum) my doctor identified the illness. If nothing else, this demonstrates how obscure it is. It is not at all obvious. When you understand depression better, it is easier to recognise it in yourself and other people.

During diagnosis, I consider that I was around I *0190* and when the initial shock had passed there was an improvement. At last I knew what was wrong with me. The enemy was exposed. Ignorance was replaced by knowledge. Also, and very notable, I had 'applied' for early retirement, which I expected would be granted. Additionally, it was springtime with all the summer to look forward to. It was a good time of year. In the summer (6.5 years on the graph) polyps were removed from my nose and I could now sleep at night with my mouth closed, relieving the discomfort of excessive dryness. Things were looking up. I retired in the summer but without much joy because I was being forced out by infirmity, which was a further loss of situation ownership; I was not leaving by choice.

In the autumn I obtained part-time employment, which supplemented my pension and gave me the impression that I was still of some use to society. The difference between compulsory and voluntary work has to be experienced to be believed. It gave me the proverbial new lease of life. Work was not a drag at all, I enjoyed it anew. With my retirement lumpsum I bought a small second house which was in considerable disrepair and I toiled on this preparatory to letting as a small additional income. I was not specially enamoured of DIY (although I had built the extension at home), but it was a novelty so I did not mind too much. On occasions I even enjoyed it a little.

The gratifyingly sharp curve of Chart *2* continued to rise until February of Year 7. I even applied for two full-time posts despite being aware that I was far too old. I thought all was well and that I was cured.

Then at some point in the Spring, the novelty wore off. Work became hard and I was grateful that my contracts were for only one year, finishing in the Summer. The house renovation became a burden. The graph plummeted, and all this occurred in the spring and summer seasons, which have always been the best part of the year for me. By September (7.75 years on **Chart** 2), I was rock- bottom; the lowest point ever. I could hardly face anybody or anything, never mind work. I think that I had attempted too much; more that I could handle. The freshness of the new circumstances had given me too much impetus and temporarily covered up the seriousness of my condition. When it resurfaced, I was finished.

A colleague at work had mentioned to me while I was still full-time, that an associate of his at a previous company had taken early retirement due to depression, and he had slept for six months afterwards. This person had appeared perfectly normal at work but he had to walk for two hours beforehand. He would get up between 5am and 6am, walk alone for a couple of hours, have his breakfast, and then go in. On retirement, he virtually collapsed. The pressure was gone, he had no need to keep going, and he slept all night and most of the day. Perhaps I should have done the same, but I did not appreciate then how ill I was.

That September I estimated that my positive/negative score was *10/90*. I was completely blown away. All I could cope with was to go for walks and potter about. From October to Christmas I took ten counselling sessions, at which I made notes. I was not the slightest bit interested in doing this but felt that I was duty bound to investigate any channel which might improve my health. I had no desire to attend, it was entirely out of deference to my doctor.

On 23rd November, in Session 6, I wrote and boxed in for emphasis *must do something physical.* At this exact moment the real recovery commenced. I have no doubt about that. I had a positive desire to go skating, I could even hear the edges cutting into the ice. I went three times before my next appointment and my counsellor was delighted and not a little amazed. So was I. I have skated regularly since then. I nearly re-joined the hockey practice and even now I might still do that.

One week later in Session 7, I inscribed *need to use brains in design capacity,* also boxed in. This thought stayed with me and, in the same way as skating gave me physical exercise, this notion produced mental exertion. It was not, however, until the latter part of the 8th year that I began this book as a project. It is a design activity. You set off with one blank piece of paper and a book takes shape. In engineering you start out with a space on the workbench and fill it with a product prototype. You plan, draw, machine, file, etc., and the approach is similar for cottage crafts or any creative work, which is inevitably stimulating. And not just creativity, because when we are engaged in anything different, we are usually more motivated than when involved in the daily routine. This can be heightened if there is just a hint of danger – in my case, skating, hockey, motor-cycling, sailing, land-yachting; for others – sky-diving, bungy jumping, etc., (but not for me, thank you). We can all find a satisfying new hobby when the urge arrives.

The graph moved gradually upwards. By the middle of February (just over 8 years) it was 15/85 which was five times better than the all-time low of the September before, but vastly inferior to the 70/30 maximum of the previous February. However, the figures were now increasing as opposed to the imminent collapse from 70/30 to almost zero.

As the spring of Year 8 progressed, my improvement continued. I had some bad days or part-days, and indeed, a poor week or two now and again, but the trend was auspicious. In fact, it might have been a bit excessive because my doctor prefers the progress to be steady rather than dramatic. I would go along with this, as a sharp rise can be superseded by an abrupt fall. The three tables featured in the previous chapter occur just before 8.5 years and the graph peaks soon after mid-summer. The ensuing decline might well be described as seasonal because the summer, which I truly enjoy, is over and autumn and winter are approaching. However, the decline soon bottomed out at 50/50 at 8.75 years and recovered to 60/40 by Easter of Year 9.

The narrative is now up to date and I am hopeful (in a very solid way which I have not experienced before during this illness) that the initial 'target' of 75125 by 9.75 years will be achieved, because there is the summer to come and I am confident that the trend from 8 to 8.75 will be repeated, although not as dramatically, from 9 to 9.75 years. With the same reasoning, I would expect 85/15 by 10.75 years, which, as far as I am concerned, is full recovery, because the 85/15 would be an average, containing some highs of total joy registering at 100/0 and some lows with correspondingly mediocre scores. Coincident with this, I would estimate that the day sleeps (which have ranged from thirty minutes to three hours) would reduce to naps of only a few minutes per day.

The total time period is really quite frightening. It means that from start to finish the illness spans ten years. For the first six the depression is concealed but eating away at mental and spiritual health and physical strength before being diagnosed. It is then another four years to recovery. In the accepted life-span of 70 years, ten years represents some fourteen per cent.

Summary

Records are used to observe and study the trend of the illness and recovery. This produces more in-depth understanding of the causes and effects of the various emotions which accompany depression.

Chapter 9
Using This Book as a Manual to Help Yourself
General Thoughts

This writing is a narrative of one person's illness and recovery interspersed with comments of a general nature. At this point in time, as mentioned earlier, I have hope. This is a substantial conviction of returning to full health. I have every confidence that the goals will be reached. However, I would emphasise that I cannot force them along. If I could then I would have done so a long time ago, but I expect the graph to get there or thereabouts, and ditto for the day sleeps. This hope materialised during a walk on February 3rd of Year 9, and it. remains with me today. I feel that I have been very, very ill and that I am fortunate to be a good way down the road to complete recovery. I do not visualise any more dramatic down-turns. I am aware of a reserve of stamina and self-confidence building up. I anticipate fluctuations in the graph, both up and down, but overall that the progress will be positive. My strength is expanding in every way – physically, mentally, and spiritually.

I would like this book to be of help to you. I know that it can be, because I am not unusual, I am the same as you. I have been seriously ill and I am now on the mend. I am not conversant with the state of your health but I am certain that the contents of the remaining chapters can assist you in formulating your own ideas to benefit your own particular condition regardless of how you may be feeling right now. If you are only on the fringes of depression at the moment, then it will be so much easier as you take the remedial action in good time. I shall offer a fair number of thoughts, and proposals for adapting them to your own needs, but what you actually do is up to you. Also, I do not want to talk down to you in a patronising way or go straight over your head. I shall try to keep it straightforward (because basically I am a simple soul) so that I can understand it, and hope that it comes out about right.

I am satisfied that it is not possible to fight your way out of deep depression but there are a number of endeavours we can undertake to facilitate recovery. I am totally convinced that we need to have a proper understanding of what has happened to us, what is happening to us now, and realistic expectations for the future. This means that we have to be in possession of past and present documentation, and some sort of estimation of when we are going to be well again. We must be able to see some light at the end of the tunnel. (I recall a dead-straight 2700-yard canal tunnel which we used to boat through near Birmingham. Without engine exhaust smoke, you could see a pin-prick of light at the other end. It took a long time to pass through the tunnel but as long as you could watch that tiny speck gradually increasing, you knew that you would eventually reach the sunshine, and how warm and welcome it was when you finally did.)

My most earnest recommendation is that you make the decision to produce some paperwork (or some more if you already have) pertaining to your illness. At the end of this paragraph, please look up from the print and make that resolve. You do not have to start the records right away, only make the decision to. Do that now, and pause for a while to think about it.

I appreciate that you may not want to help yourself. Depression is negative. Deep depression is exceedingly, if not totally, negative. However, we all have a duty to make what effort we can to keep going. I suggest that you continue reading to the end of the final chapter and then study the whole book again (it is not very long) with pen and paper at your side. Make some notes as you go along. You may decide to buy an exercise book or use loose pages in a folder. Make sure you number the pages and date every entry. You will find that you refer to them frequently and you will want to know when this and that and the other actually occurred. Once you get started, you will discover that you are able to take an interest (albeit a detached one) in the state and movement of your condition. I found this, so you will, as well.

The written work that you are going to tackle is not a one-off to get it out of the way. It is a daily routine. It may only require five minutes of your time; but you may spend longer. You will be assembling a dossier. You will be gaining knowledge and understanding, which exposes the enemy. Thoughts may come to you at odd times during the day when you are out walking, shopping, etc. If you carry a pen and a piece of folded A4 paper with you, you can jot down the key words and amplify them later. I cannot over-emphasise how vitally important my records have been, and are, to me. I know that I would not be anywhere near as far along the path to full health without them. If I had read a book such as this one, before or in the early stages of my illness, then I would not have been so unwell.

Summary

We need to appreciate how and why we have arrived in our present situation in order that we can plan for full recovery, this requires documentation so that we can study and ponder without having to rely on a mental picture, which may be changeable and even faulty due to poor memory.

Chapter 10
Specific Suggestions to Assist You in Your Own Recovery or Prevention Programme

What I would like to do now is to list a whole collection of ideas for your consideration. Most of them are extracted from my written records and are feelings or thoughts which were with me at the time. In the final chapter we will summarise the salient points and discuss how they may be useful when adapted to your own particular case. This is a long chapter which I hope (and expect) will be useful to you. Here we go.

1. Written records (have you heard that before?) are not really optional, they are vital.

2. See your doctor. You might think this is futile but, in my view, can be very productive. When I visited my Dr Y, I had no concept of how much she would do for me. I did not know beforehand that all the following would happen over the months and years: diagnosis, expedition of removal of nose polyps, letter to back-up early retirement request, letter to reinforce sickness claim to insurance company, assistance with other benefits, continuous understanding and encouragement, no hassle when anti-depressants not used, support for homeopathic (minimal or no side effects) alternative remedies, suggestion of and assistance with part-time 'therapeutic' work,

recommendation and arrangement of counselling, and I am sure there is more. All these contributed to a greater or lesser extent to the recovery, the most important being the first. Without accurate identification, you cannot even start to get better.

Prepare a written report when you go for your appointment. This should be succinct but still contain the important features. You know what these are, and when they are written down, you will not forget them. These notes will be a valuable part of your records. Otherwise there will be no account of your progress for you or your doctor.

Because my doctor seems to appreciate the written assessments which I take along with me, I enclose one below. This was for February of Year 8. It is reproduced almost verbatim.

Assessment February
Positive Characteristics:

- Ice skating twice per week as a result of counselling sessions.
- Morning of 25th January 100/0 – brilliant.
- Feel quite good for a few minutes several times per week.
- Aiming to work in September.
- 2nd February visited Company and chatted to staff. Felt quite good and September feels realistic (if any work available). *[At this juncture, I will answer the obvious question – "Why do you want to work when you have taken early retirement?" I was forced to leave work because of ill health and I would like to make my own decisions, as we all do, and not have them imposed on me situation ownership again. I expected to retire at 60 years of age or soon after, and I was determined to work again so that the finishing date was resolved of my own free will and choice.]*

- Marginally more motivated now. Enjoy skating. Want to use brains (but very little stamina and cannot get going yet).
- Generally, not too bothered about illness, feel that recovery will happen.
- Feel that over the worst, and this if current 'lifestyle' continued, will eventually get good health again.
- Feel less 'guilty' at being unable to work. Appreciate that have serious illness, even though intangible.

Negative Characteristics:-

- Sleep in chair for at least one hour (sometimes 2 or even 3 hours) most afternoons.
- Worry about anything extra or unusual. Start yawning a lot.
- Could not go to work at the moment.
- Not much stamina, mental or physical.
- Small tasks take a long time, a lot of effort, dither about, and then tired.
- Short-term memory problems.
- Black periods still black. Very bad Christmas day. Feel completely drained and burned out.
- Sometimes (not very often) zero motivation for anything.
- Still need to walk out-of-doors in daylight, preferably sunshine. Minimum 1.5 hours per day.
- Still easily discouraged. If too much bother, just walk away. Put off till another day.

Conclusion:

- Improvement since last September.
- Hopefully able to work and able to obtain work in September.

This occupied one side of an A4 sheet, which, I would think, is sufficient. It then became part of my health diary.

3. Check your diet. You may want to involve your doctor with this. There are plenty of diet books available in libraries and book shops. We need to drink enough fluids. Tea, coffee and alcohol are now generally accepted as not good for us. You could try non-toxic drinks such as orange and other squashes (with hot or cold water), fruit juices, malt beverages, etc. Tobacco is also bad for you, physically and financially. Eat meat sparingly. Eat fresh fruit, wheat products and fresh vegetables. Supplementary vitamins may be beneficial. Take an interest in what you eat.

4. There is an old saying that we need plenty of exercise and plenty of rest. Do you get enough? As you exercise and then rest, you attain a sense of well-being. This usually means that more than a gentle stroll is requisite. There is another expression – no pain, no gain – but be careful. Here a little, there a little; make progress gradually. Consult your doctor and the many physical fitness publications obtainable. Early to bed and early to rise makes sense. Late night films and sleeping in the following morning will not make us feel good, neither will watching most day-time television.

5. You might like to investigate alternative medicine. There is an abundance of literature and practitioners at the moment. I have personal experience of the efficacy of the correct homeopathic remedy. For years my nose was runny and only a nasal spray could dry it up. By chance, my wife recommended a remedy and overnight it cured it. The ones I took for depression helped a bit, I felt, but were not dramatic

like that. Still, any relief is always welcome and contributes to the overall cure.

There are many different types of alternative treatments for health improvement.

6. Chapter 6 is a brief discourse on 'religion'. You may well have you own views on this subject. Personally, I need the truth and am grateful that I am in possession of it. Without the rock of the Gospel, I could not have survived. Indeed, there would appear to be no point in struggling on or even existing unless you can see where you are in the overall plan, which is being managed by a caring God, who knows the end from the beginning, and who is one hundred per cent fair. I recommend plenty of pondering and prayer. *"Seek and ye shall find."* Personally, I walk in the countryside (whenever possible) to do this. Afterwards write down how you feel (as appropriate) as an addition to your records, which you can study again later, otherwise you may forget.

7. Take counselling sessions with a professional whom you have not met before, and make notes. Because the meetings were so useful to me, I include them much as I wrote them during the meetings with the counsellor.

Each one is followed by a comment written during the production of this book.

Session 1

What is objective? More understanding, release feelings, improvement in health.

What is expected outcome after the 10 weeks? What have been other clients' experiences?

Depression and anxiety caused by work stress. Does rest help with cure? Yes.

Does enforced work help? No. Some work? Different work?

Duty? Mother's death? Children growing up?

Comment on 1

I was trying to see what use the counselling might be. We had a discussion about work and whether it would be good or bad for the depression (academic really as I was too ill to face anything). At that time, I had been retired for just over a year and was at my lowest level ever. I was not happy with retirement. I would preferably have been at work and well, rather than at home and ill. Perhaps I was undergoing a sense of guilt at not working – mention of duty? We then moved on to other possible causes of depression. I remember little of the counselling meetings and, as you can see, my notes were brief and haphazard.

Session 2

Felt much better last Saturday. Is this because it is not a working day? Still not motivated to do anything.

Suppressed feelings – one suppressed feeling can hold down others as well.

Anger or sadness at no notice being taken of ideas at work? One pivotal feeling can affect other feelings.

Losses – father going away to war, unavailability of mother after birth of youngest brother, loss of baby, miscarriage, grandmother dies, father dies, mother dies, work loss due to depression, financial loss, perceived poor management at work, current government, poor opposition management, lack of integrity, loss of little children (as they grow up).

Loss is always a component in depression. Anxiety?

Comment on 2

The counsellor must have broached the subject of loss and I noted some of her ideas and some of mine. We all experience misfortune as we go through life, and usually we withstand it.

However, either a combination of losses or a sustained loss over a long period can finally bring us down.

The important aspect is that I became engaged in thought processes with which I would not have bothered without the counselling sessions. They awakened and stimulated contemplation which otherwise might not have ever (or for a long time anyway) occurred.

Session 3
Anxiety – more obvious as agitation. Depression – suppression of feelings.

Sadness – counsellor senses this during silences. I may be sorrowing for 'the sins of the world'.

Look at areas of enrichment, and areas where there is no longer any enrichment.

Comment on 3
Presumably we were discussing depression and anxiety, and I was attempting to differentiate between them. This was covered a bit more in Chapter 2. The sadness comment was perceptive – I did feel sad, albeit obliviously. She also used 'enrichment', which is a significant word. Depression robs us of joy, and my counsellor was suggesting that I recall those facets of my life where there was still enrichment and then those where it had faded or vanished.

Session 4
Prescription.

Post-viral fatigue.

Areas of enrichment – holiday feeds a spiritual need
– Temple feeds a spiritual need
– walking in daylight in countryside
– ice skating
– motor-cycling
– dinghy sailing
– land-yachting

I do NOT want to work. Rephrase. I am not motivated – I would like to want to work.

Have I had enough of duty?

What would I like to do with no restrictions? I feel guilty at being the only one at home.

Comment on 4

I had been given a new prescription which I was worried about, so we discussed it, and then my excessive lethargy. We continued the topic of the week before with areas of enrichment, which are all leisure activities. I was still involved with the first three, but the remaining four had ceased. This was followed by a discussion about work, which I had generally enjoyed except for my view of management attitudes mentioned earlier in this book. The word 'restriction' appears. This is when situation ownership is being curtailed. I do not believe that it is good for us to be completely unrestricted so that we suit ourselves all the time. We all benefit from some guidelines and tuition to be about our duty, but excess leads to unrighteous dominion, which profits nobody. I think that my sense of guilt at being the only one at home originated from my early retirement, even though it was constrained by ill-health. If I had been over 60, I do not believe that I would have felt badly at all about this particular aspect.

Session 5

Physical effects of depression?

There is a physiological component in depression, e.g., women after child-birth, menopause, etc. This may be hormones.

My prescription is chemical changes to the brain.

Sports and shouting can release anger. This would be a healthy release. Fear with exhilaration could be part of this. Involuntary intake of breath may have come after the 'release' but no release yet perhaps.

Have I overridden feelings by being competent, practical, and supportive?

Am I getting lost in duty?

Comment on 5

A few words about the physical side of depression. There is no doubt that bodily exertion tinged with an appropriate (in my case only minuscule) amount of danger culminates in elation and a sense of well-being. I do not understand the sentence about intake of breath, which I listed as a symptom in the first chapter. During the meetings, I occasionally noted the counsellor's remarks without fully comprehending them. Duty crops up again and the implication was that my sense of duty, which is very strong, might have repressed certain emotions and thus contributed to depression. I never took the prescription because I had no wish for any alterations to my brain.

Session 6

Suppressed feelings – anger, pleasure, irritation, sadness, grief, joy, love, hate, fear, anxiety, excitement, guilt, enthusiasm.

Counsellor has sensed sadness which is almost inevitably due to loss.

As not working i.e., duty – cannot allow pleasure?

Lost capacity for service to little children, and also in work. Enthusiasm had gone. Guilt might be the cause.

Have not earned pleasure through service. MUST DO SOMETHING PHYSICAL.

Comment on 6

We listed various emotions which can be suppressed, and sadness reappears. Duty is cited again and also lack of enthusiasm. The 'little children' sentence refers to my own children growing up. Finally, and I do not remember how it arose, I had the desire to get some exercise (walking at my pace does not really count). Perhaps some memory of the good times which I had enjoyed in sporting activities returned fleetingly, and I wanted to revive them. Whatever it was, I am satisfied that this was the turning point. I reinstated ice skating and from then on progress has been positive even though there have been inevitable minor local fluctuations.

Session 7

Boredom? Sexual feelings?

Has counsellor met cases similar to mine? What was/is outcome? Does she get feedback?

When tracing suppressed feeling, how far back do we have to go?

Nothing more creative at work? Same old job? NEED TO USE BRAINS IN DESIGN CAPACITY.

Need a structure as in work.

Comment on 7

There was a brief discussion of the effects of boredom and sexual attitudes. I recall that I introduced the latter because of the once popular notion that most, if not all, psychological conditions can be traced to sexual disturbances (Mr. Freud was it?). I do not remember her answer so perhaps current theories have moderated. We then reverted to the subject of work and I wrote the sentence in capital letters and the last one containing 'structure'. Within two months (8.25 years on **Chart 1**) I was keeping my own detailed medical records, and giving my life some more formal organisation, e.g. 'work' hours. At 8.75 years I embarked on three months of paid part-time employment and this book was begun in outline soon afterwards. This constituted the inauguration of mental recovery to complement the physical restoration of Session 6 above.

Session 8

Important to work with or be with people who have a sense of humour.

Add fun and humour to 'feelings' page of Session 6. Add these to jobs profile. Bring this next week.

Think of reasons why it is ok to be retired early
  – younger people get jobs
  – can find other things to do
  – entitled to a rest

Work with little children could be important. Teach juniors?

Comment on 8

This session is a blank to me. We must have re-examined, expressed and suppressed feelings, and a new one – humour – surfaced. I am a Brummie (native of Birmingham), where there is a considerable amount of banter. When we moved south to a more rural location, I was surprised at the dearth of repartee in most of the population, both native and move-ins. I do miss the Brummie wit. Work was back on the agenda and I had vague thoughts that it would be nice to teach little children instead of adults. I had enjoyed this very much when I was assigned a Primary class at Church, and my own little ones had brought me so much joy.

Session 9

Have I lost my childhood?
Does the child in me need to get out?
Is there a bridge between children and engineering?
Talking about children could have significance at Christmas time?
Characteristics of 'ideal' job – physical, brains, boss, part-time, technical, useful, not isolated, motor-cycle, from home, outdoors, sailing, Gloucester, children?

Comment on 9

The first four questions look like fairly heavy psychological ones posed by my counsellor and they do not mean a lot to me. The job profile was just thoughts that came to me. I cannot imagine what sort of employment would contain all those features! Nonetheless, I was at least involved in some sort of deliberation. I think that Gloucester was a feature because it is reasonably central (for the Midlands) and I could sail on the Severn river (which I had done many years before, but higher upstream).

Session 10

Losses and 'gains' – current
                            – positive future events to look forward
                            to.

September Year six to February Year seven felt much better. This could happen again.

Comment on 10

The counselling took place on Wednesday afternoons and this meeting was on the Wednesday before Christmas Day on the Sunday, so there was not much momentum. The useful work had already been done (although the full effects were yet many months away) and we were both pleased that this was the final session.

8. Express your feelings. Suppression of emotions is generally bad for us and if we deliberately 'bottle' them up, then eventually the bottle will explode. It may be that your nearest and dearest are the best people to whom you divulge all your troubles. It may be that they are the worst, and tell you to shut up and pull yourself together. I favour an unknown and completely impartial counsellor. You can be absolutely honest and talk about anything at all. The chances are that they will not offer any specific advice, mine made none (that I can recall), but I was enabled to reach my own conclusions, which instigated my recovery.

My counselling was under the auspices of the N.H.S., so it cost me nothing {I know we all have to contribute in taxes, national insurance, etc.) and I was allowed ten sessions. I think that if any more had been necessary then I would have had to pay myself, and I believe it is quite expensive. I think that you can contact volunteer 'amateur' organisations, such as the Samaritans, any time. You might have a friend (you may need care here) or Church member who will listen, and sometimes, just voicing your distress can bring relief.

You can always find somewhere to be alone or go for a walk and commune with your God or simply with yourself. As long as the feelings are asserted, they will tend to be disarmed. You cannot go around telling everyone to their face what you think of them in a derogatory manner. They will likely not appreciate it, and you may find that they retaliate warmly to give you even more grief. However, on your own, you should be all right. Be honest. Mere repetition of 'I don't really mind that so and so is upsetting me' etc. will not improve matters; it will contribute to the suppression and the inevitable explosion when you cannot keep the lid on any longer. Be brutally frank and bring the true sentiments out into the open. Then you may well find that you can eventually generate a satisfactory solution. This may even be possible without upsetting anybody. There are plenty of books on this subject. Have a browse in your local library and book shops.

9.   Set some targets. You have to be realistic here and be prepared to reduce them without being despondent if you set them too high initially. It is not the same as goal-setting when you are fit. In that event you might, for instance, determine to jog for an hour per day within, say, six months. You run along your first route, which might take ten minutes, for two weeks, and then increase it so that you keep going for 15 minutes. By your own efforts you build up to 60 minutes within the prescribed period. This cannot be accomplished with depression because you cannot control how you will respond. If you could, you would, and nobody would ever suffer from this affliction.

However, you can give yourself an objective and see how you get on. For instance, at 8.75 years I set a goal of three-quarters recovery (with its definitions) for 9.75 years, and full recovery (also defined) by 10.75 years. I am of the opinion that these are realistically attainable but I shall not be upset if they are not reached. They are to be hoped for but I cannot guarantee them. However, I can always redesignate them and have another go.

You can also aim for short-term objectives, which are attained more quickly and can be measured more precisely. I went back to skating and sailing, and I intend to continue them. I sought some part-time work and managed to sustain it until the end of the contract. I plan to be fit for full-time employment. I propose to finish this book whether or not it is published. I have allocated a number of hours for writing, revising, word- processing, etc., per week at home on an increasing scale over a fixed time period. Initially it was too optimistic, and had to be 'downsized', but I was not discouraged. I was, after all, actually doing something.

I recommend that you try some immediate and future goal- setting. Immediate might be to go for one or two walks every day, or so many per week, or walk to the shops for the daily newspaper, or read a new book for an hour or more each day, or write for half-an-hour, etc. It does not matter how simple your targets are. The object is to get well. To paraphrase the American (I think) football coach – "Winning (in our case, full recovery) is not everything, it is the only thing." We cannot surgically remove the depression, or we would, but we can take some simple actions to help ourselves. Every oak tree starts as a little acorn. Long-term ambitions can be equally modest but will be some months if not years (but not too many) ahead.

10. Take a dispassionate look at the origin of stress in your life. I am a firm believer that a certain amount of pressure is good for us; for example, setting goals can do this, but excess can undoubtedly bring on depression. The balance is absolutely critical. Too much can result in serious illness, too little definitely produces lethargy and stifling boredom. This, I suppose, could be a stress factor in itself, though whether it could result in depression is beyond my experience. I know a successful businessman who had previously been one of many technicians in a large organisation until the monotony drove him to look elsewhere and start up his own. In my case the tension originated mainly from my particular employment, but retirement did not result in instant

release from depression because it had, by then, penetrated too deeply.

If there is too much stress in your life, then you need to shed some. It was my fortune to be able to retire. If it had occurred ten years earlier, when I was in my forties, it would not have been so easy. If you are in a pressure situation from which you cannot walk away (and we all have them) for whatever reason, what should you do?

It is essential to locate the underlying cause(s). It may be unmistakable – bad management, bad marriage, etc., or it may be concealed. It may be hidden in the past. Here again, you will need notes. Write down all possibilities, however unlikely they may be. Then ponder carefully about each one. Whenever you have a thought, jot it down. The process may take hours, days, weeks, but you must establish the real complaint(s). You can then determine what troubles you can discard and what you are stuck with.

There is a theory that there are only two types of problem – the one that you can do something about – and the one that you can do nothing about. The premise is that you do what you can about the first, and forget about the second because it is beyond your control. Personally, I do not subscribe to this because you can always choose your response to any situation, however abhorrent it may be. Attitude is the answer to everything.

There is a very moving story about a survivor of one of those terrible concentration camps of the last world war. His liberators found that this man's appearance and demeanour was markedly better than those of his fellow-inmates, and they presumed that he had benefited from special privileges. Further investigation revealed that this was not the case. He had been taken to the camp with his family to be eliminated, but his captors discovered that he possessed fluent language skills which would be useful to them. They shot his family, but not him, despite his pleas to die with them. This incredible person then decided that he was through with hate, and he cultivated an attitude of love towards all mankind. This not only kept him alive but also accounted for his outstanding appearance among the other poor souls. He differentiated between behaviour and people. We are allowed to disapprove of behaviour but we should love the person. There is a proverb – hate the sin, love the sinner.

This man's perspective was breath-taking. How do we foster ours in our relatively much less severe circumstances? There is undoubtedly a universal answer and surely it must be based on the experience of this great man, but we are now in the realms of personal response. I know where I turn for my salvation (see Chapter 6), for me it is the only place to go, but we all have to make our own decisions. We can all choose a course of action and then we have to accept the unavoidable consequences. We make the initial selection but we cannot choose the outcome, so it is advisable to do our best to get it right.

Earlier we discussed where stress might occur in our lives – work, family, leisure, health – and these same domains are where we can also have great satisfaction. You might care to consider each of these in turn and estimate the relative worries and joys.

This may assist you in arriving at a proper solution, which, unless you are very fortunate, may take a considerable amount of time and effort – but it can be done.

11. Do something different. Is there something you would have liked to do, but never did? Can you change your work, family activities, leisure activities, your health outlook? If you are unable to alter these dramatically, can you become involved in additional pursuits which will provide you with interest and perhaps a bit more money? Hobbies can often bring in income. Our successful technician started his business on a part-time basis, and there are many other similar winners. There are books and magazines replete with ideas for making money from home (but beware of cowboys, there are plenty about). Can you

institute new family or leisure enterprises? These might well be combined.

A word of warning here. The most important task is to determine why you feel as you do. It is no use masking the illness with your endeavour as happened to me with ice-skating, hockey and the extension. We are looking for a cure, not a cloak. Once you understand why you are ill you can then institute appropriate treatment, which might well involve some diverse activities.

12. Use spiritual aids to recovery. If your religion helps you, then use it. I personally favour absolute truth. This is not dependent on anybody's deeply-felt, totally sincere beliefs. It stands alone as factual knowledge. One fact is that there is a God who hears prayers and grants us that which is expedient for us, from his knowledge of all things from the beginning to the end.

One spiritual 'tool' is fasting. The effect is greatly amplified when combined with prayer. Fasting consists of abstaining from food and liquid for 24 hours (lunchtime one day until lunchtime the next day is my preferred interval). It should not be practised excessively. Once a month should be sufficient but check with your doctor if necessary. Scripture study is also beneficial, as is complying with the Saviour's precepts found therein. Even if these ideas sound novel to you, have a go, you can only profit by it.

13. Get your brain moving. We all need mental stimulation as well as physical labour. Try to make the effort to do some sort of study – write an article for a magazine, enrol on a course at your local college and pass an exam to obtain a qualification, write a journal of your life, research your ancestors and compile your family history, join a local society or job club or voluntary group, invent something, visit

your library more, etc. We all have a duty to use the talents we have been given. Turn your television off.

14. Address problems. I know this is tiresome when there is little or no motivation but, generally, the thought of having to tackle a task is worse than the task itself. Once you are underway you find that you keep going and the problem is overcome. Write down your troubles. They may be trivial – dripping tap, leaking shed, broken window; or very serious – family relationships, work complications, etc. As a rule, they do not go away on their own, so make a start on them. Once a weight is moving the effort to drag it is less. You need only provide the initial effort; the remainder will often follow automatically.

I remarked earlier in Chapter 5 that I constructed a single-storey extension to the back of our house. Although it camouflaged the depression, there were some very positive aspects which I would like to relate in the context of making a start and watching how things seem to progress all on their own.

I had never previously undertaken a task of this magnitude (I am aware that it is all in a day's work for a builder), but I knew that I was quite capable of digging the trench for the foundations. All you need is a spade to shift the dirt (in my case heavy clay, but at least it enabled the children to supply the school with modelling material for quite some time). Once the inspector had passed the earthworks, I decided that I could shovel ready-mix concrete as well as the next person and we put it in as a family activity. My bricklaying capabilities were almost zero but the initial block work would be underground so I could experiment without regard to the appearance. By the time the blocks were above ground level, the work looked quite respectable. I read books, asked advice, and eventually the room was finished apart from a small amount of internal plastering, which I contracted out. I contemplate the room now with some amazement that I was able to do it. It all started with the right approach and a spade.

The resolution of any difficulty may be a long way off but you will feel better for venturing out in the first place. There is always an answer. Sometimes all you can do is to develop the optimum attitude but this in itself may bring peace of mind, which, in fact, could be the sought-after solution.

15. Make a plan for life. This may sound a bit overwhelming but you do not have to accomplish it all in one day. Generally speaking, we cannot see the end from the beginning (unlike our God, who can), and we are moving towards the unknown. When we are healthy this does not worry us. Consciously or unconsciously we presume that since we have come this far and weathered life's dilemmas, so we will handle any others as they arise. When we have depression, we lose our confidence and the future unsettles us because we do not know what will strike us next. Nonetheless, as problems arise, we are compelled to make decisions.

Years ago, when computers were at an early stage of development, a common language used to program them was called Basic. This was relatively easy because it was much like writing in the English language (providing you spoke English, that is). There was a conditional instruction known as 'IF, THEN', which enabled the programmer to build in future decision-making capability into the computer. He might write:

- Line 20 If y less than 200, THEN go to Line 1000. Perhaps y is the number of seats on an aeroplane with a maximum capacity of 200 passengers. At line 1000 there might be an instruction to post the seat reservation to the client, because the plane is not yet full. The next line after 20 could be:
- Line 30 If y equal to or greater than 201 THEN go to Line 1020:

At line 1020, there could be a directive to inform the client that the plane was fully booked and to provide an alternative. There is no need for the booking team to worry whether the seats are all taken because a plan of action has already been thought out.

Your plan for life, your philosophy for living, will contain responses to certain situations which may occur in the future. You then face the decisions before they are actually needed, so that you know what to do should they in reality crop up. This means that you can sort yourself out at leisure instead of panicking when the pressure appears and your time to react is limited by events. By previewing possible events you keep the ownership of the situation. This puts your mind to rest.

I will briefly recount my own experience. When I was very ill but unaware of my condition, I had some thoughts concerning early retirement. My main interest was financial because our three children were still at school. The conditional clauses were along the following lines:

- IF I retire now THEN my pension will be £A per annum. My family currently requires £B per annum. This leads to a shortfall of £(B-A). However, my lump sum is £C.
- IF I do no work THEN we can last out C/(B-A) years with current expenditure. By then our family ages will be whatever. However, our outgoings can be reduced.
- IF we reduce expenditure THEN we can continue another D year. Also, although gross income will be less than at present, net income will not suffer as much because there will be no superannuation or National Insurance contributions.
- IF I do some work THEN we can keep going longer.
- IF my wife stays with her job THEN longer again.

This and more filled about three sides of A4 paper, which I carried with me in my back pocket, and I pondered and added to them.

Curiously enough, my most important resolve took place when I was a young man in my mid-twenties. I had observed the decline of two colleagues, one older than me, and the other, my own age. They both became ill with depression, although in those days it was designated mental breakdown. I remarked to another colleague, who was as young and fit as I was, that if ever my work made me ill, then I would get out. He thought this might not be possible for various reasons but I insisted that I would leave whatever the cost. I never wrote this down anywhere but it remained with me over the years. I always preserved (subconsciously, I suppose) that decision, which was reinforced as I saw others 'go down' during my working life.

Accordingly, it was no surprise that when my doctor diagnosed depression, the first words I spoke after I stopped crying were that I would leave my current job. My doctor suggested that perhaps there was no need to take such a drastic step, but I repeated to her what I had always said – that if my work made me ill then I would finish with it. The health of the breadwinner and parent is of paramount importance. It is a matter of simple priority. You are not much help to your family if you are ill, and no use at all if you are dead. Insurance may cover financial loss but your dependants are still without your guiding companionship, which they will most likely miss desperately, even though you may not think that.

Fortunately, early retirement fell into my lap, but I would have gone anyway. The management were surprised at my instant decision – "why not think about it for a while?" – but, in reality, it had been made for a long time.

I recommend a plan for life, a plan for survival – long-term or short-term. Anticipate the options that may come your way. Face them without pressure before they occur. If you wait until the wolf is actually at the door you are more prone to mistakes because you may panic. Cross your bridges before you come to them. Sort things out at leisure in advance, you will find that it will pay off enormously.

16. Be flexible in your response. You may initiate a policy and then find that you cannot complete it. Not to worry, manage what you can. Down-grade your schedule until it is realisable, you can always upgrade it later. There is no need for concern if your strategy changes completely. As long as you have a record, you can see why. Schemes evolve. As you meditate there is a polarising effect and you decide on a course of action, which is probably right at that particular time. As conditions alter, so does your plan. You will probably recognise the final draft because it will feel right to you. You will feel settled in your mind, but still be prepared to be adaptable.

You might wonder if always being prepared for change leads to instability. You might prefer a programme which never alters. There is one such called the Plan of Salvation as we touched on in Chapter 6. We can rely on the rock of the Saviour. He never changes, his course is one eternal round. He is the same yesterday, today, and forever. Relying on the arm of Jehovah, as the scriptures advise, leads to stability in a global or strategic sense, but our local tactics in everyday life still need to be flexible.

Summary

This is a very long chapter. There follows an abstract of the suggestions for positive steps to assist you in the recovery process. These are not exhaustive. Use whatever you think will help you, plus, of course, your own ideas.

1. Written records – essential.
2. See your doctor.
3. Check your diet.
4. Exercise and rest.
5. Alternative medicines.

6. Religion.
7. Counselling.
8. Express your feelings (with care) – essential.
9. Set goals.
10. Find the origin of your stress –essential.
Attitude – essential.

11. Do something different.
12. Spiritual aids to recovery.
13. Get your brain moving.
14. Address problems.
15. Plan for life.
16. Be flexible.

I have exercised all these myself and I am on the mend. I am confident of regaining very good health. The most important feature for me personally is *number 6,* without which there is no point in being well, or indeed, in being. Other than this, *number 10* must be the top priority – attitude is the key to recovery in the same way as loss of situation ownership is the cause of all depression.

Chapter 11

A Few Thoughts for Those People Concerned About Someone Else with or Approaching Depression

You may be reading this book because you are worried that someone you know may be suffering from depression (indeed, it may already have been diagnosed), and you are looking for some guidance as to how you can help. In fact, the first person to study the initial draft did so for this very reason, and this chapter has been produced at her request. It contains my conjectures both as a sufferer and as a struggling mentor, which I would have found exceedingly frustrating if I had not been in possession of the extra insight gained from first-hand personal affliction.

What you tend to do is to analyse the patient's situation and then come up with your own solution, which you think is a very good one. For instance, it would obviously be good for him (please read her as appropriate) to have an evening out at the theatre, so you buy the tickets and present them with great enthusiasm. You explain what a good performance it is (the reviews have been excellent and you have friends who have been and really enjoyed it) and how you can both go for a meal afterwards. It will be a really good evening.

The depressive says, "No thanks, I don't want to go." You are somewhat taken aback. How could anybody refuse this wonderful opportunity? So, you try again. You reiterate how super it will be and how beneficial for the patient. It will obviously be good for him, what is the matter with him?

Eventually his negativism wins the day and you retreat, angry and hurt.

It is extremely exasperating and disappointing. Whatever you suggest, and they are most likely helpful recommendations, he just does not want to co-operate. To compound your discomfort, he may well be terse and irritable and not show any inclination to be helped, and there is no way that you can jolly him out of it. In fact, he is impossible. So, what can you do?

You can realise that, although there is nothing obvious to show it, he is in reality suffering from a very serious illness, which is not going to disappear simply because you think that you know how to put it right. Rapid recovery will not occur just because you are nice to him and put up with his ungracious behaviour. A man with a broken leg cannot play football and that is how it is. You could dress him in his kit and carry him to the pitch but he cannot play however much you exhort him. It is a physical impossibility. He would undoubtedly oblige you if he could, but he cannot. There are also mental impossibilities but there is no plaster cast for you to see, so it is easy for you to think that he is not really ill, but he is. I imagine that you will feel anger and despair on occasions.

A broken leg will usually heal in a matter of weeks; depression may be over in a matter of months or years, hopefully not too many; it depends on how deep it is. However, you can be confident that the chances for full recovery are good. Until then, you will, unfortunately, need a lot of patience. By all means make suggestions but pushing them overly hard will probably only wear you out as well, and he is worn out already, poor beggar.

A college student was one day bemoaning that he did not understand an engineering principle which his lecturer had been expounding. I happened to know this teacher, who was an obliging enough person in his day, so I suggested to the student that he might ask him again. "I did", was the reply, "And he told me exactly the same thing, only louder."

Likewise, if you keep repeating the same unwanted advice, it likely will not help matters, neither will criticism.

You could ask questions and accept the answers, even though they may not be what you want to hear.

"Would you like to go to the theatre?"

"No thanks."

This does not mean that he will always refuse, but today, no thanks. Ask him again on another day.

"What do you want to do tonight?" –

"Nothing."

You could be more specific and mention the activities which he used to enjoy. There might be a spark left. He might reject everything. Depression is negative. Keep the broken leg in your mind.

"Do you want a holiday? A new car? A hobby?"

When you have done your best, let it be. Think about his responses. You may find a key somewhere. When he has a good day or a good part of a day, do not get too excited. It might be an isolated incident, but anything positive is a good sign. You could put it in your medical record or his medical record with a comment. It might be useful in the future. Try to date everything and even the time to obtain some sort of perspective.

I do not recall the precise stimulus during my counselling which caused me to write *must do something physical* and box it in for emphasis, but I thought it, and I wrote it, not my counsellor; but I very much doubt if this would have occurred if she had not been talking with me. Even if I could remember the precise details, they might well only apply to me; some other mechanism may probably be needed for your situation, so do not give up, keep talking. ·

Watch out for warning signs for yourself. If you are very close to the patient, the state of affairs could start to get you down as well. If you think that you know why he is in depression, do not tell him directly; see if you can set the scene so that he realises for himself (always assuming that you were right in the first place). It may not be pleasant for him (or you) and he might not want to acknowledge it, but we have to be honest. For instance, there may be financial hardship ahead, the job may have to go and the next one may not pay so much.

How can stress be reduced? Take it steadily. Think about it. The chances are that something has to change or he will continue downhill. What changes are necessary? There is probably no instant solution. Anti-biotics fight the infection wherever it is. This is much more complex. There may be the equivalent of several different infections, each requiring different treatment, and even the medication may have to evolve as the recovery progresses. It is a day-at-a-time process, you may have to see what each day brings. Planning precisely for the future may not be easy, it may not even be possible at first. You will most likely have to "think on your feet". My recovery was not often orderly, it was up and down a lot as the tables show. However, I always believed in complete recovery eventually, and it did come, eventually. It will too for you, or the one you care about, but it is hard work.

Summary

Realise that the illness is very serious.

Realise that you cannot enforce a cure but you can help (with care).

Realise that you are going to need a lot of patience.

Realise that recovery is very likely, indeed, almost certain.

Chapter 12

Final Summary

Recommended Procedures When Reading Through This Book Again

This concluding chapter reviews all the previous chapters with additional comments on what you might do as the first stage in clarifying your own state of health. I did not know that I was ill, and you may be in a somewhat similar situation in that you do not feel right but you cannot put your finger on what is wrong.

I advise you to reread from the beginning with pen and paper at your side because the chances of uncovering what is happening to you without a written record must be very low, so make notes. Follow the suggestions, answer the questions and any others that come to mind. Once you get started, the rest will follow. I began this book with one sheet of paper and a vague idea. It soon multiplied (which may or may not delight you!).

Chapter 1 – Depression can be exceedingly serious and yet not apparent to the sufferer. What is your personal condition? Study the nineteen related symptoms. Do they describe you? If so, what is the frequency and magnitude of them? Do you have others not listed here which could be relevant? Are they new to you? If not new, are they becoming more intense? You are aiming to find out how ill you are, so think hard, it is important. This is not a questionnaire in a magazine for your amusement. This is of grave importance. Depression is not an ailment to be regarded lightly even though people who do not suffer from it may do so. Your deliberations may last several days or even longer. Jot down any thoughts that come to you and rearrange them carefully later. Note your feelings – positive and negative (probably mostly the latter).

Chapter 2 – Anxiety is apparently a separate medical issue, although I doubt if the patient is much concerned about the precise name of his affliction. More symptoms are discussed. You may have recorded these already from the previous chapter. They are all stress related.

Before long, you will have most of your diagnosis completed and you can then gather the information into a short report for your doctor, who will have hard-copy evidence in front of him, which is easier than deciphering your verbal account. He will also see that you are taking an earnest interest in your health. At this stage there is no reason to worry about solutions. You may think that you are in an impossible situation which cannot be resolved, but you need only take one step at a time. Right now, you are into diagnosis, the answers will materialise in due course.

Chapter 3 – Depression is caused by stress. We all have stress in our lives and indeed some can probably even be beneficial. What we can manage without is prolonged pressure, and we definitely need to discover its origin. You may already have an impression lurking in the back of your mind but you do not want to face it. However, it has to be done some time, go for it now.

Write down the main areas in your life – work, family, leisure – and health, and any others, and note any possible (even if unlikely) sources of stress. As you do so, take notice of your emotions, particularly resentment or sadness. Consider your general health, what feelings do you have about this? The first two chapters may lead you to believe that you have depression in some degree, this current exercise is to analyse why this should be.

Chapter 4 – The underlying cause of all depression is too much stress brought about by loss of situation ownership.

Record which parts of your life you have control over (proactive – you can decide what to do) and which parts you do not govern (reactive – you can only respond to events). Consider the areas of the previous chapter and any others which might be significant. Note your feelings. We are still examining why. You need as much information as possible about your condition so that you can understand what is happening to you, and why you feel like you do.

Chapter 5 – This is an objective history of my own depression. You need to compile an account of yours. Use whatever time scale you think is requisite for your own Chart 1. I started with two points – one when I knew that I was well – and the other when I was certain that I was ill. I then designated the mid- point of these as the beginning of the depression. Put your own time scale down on paper together with any salient features – good and bad memories, gains and losses, work events, holidays, family land-marks, etc. You may require more than one chart. One might cover a time span of many years. The other could expand particular sections of this as you begin to delve into the critical regions. Do not rush this and do not hesitate to modify it as ideas come to you.

Chapter 6 – A brief outline of the importance of knowing where I fit into the eternal blueprint of existence. This is available to all who seek it.

Chapter 7 – Similar to Chapter 5. A record of my road to recovery. You will also travel along your own route to good health. It needs to be chronicled because trends must be established if you are to observe your development. I did this by converting feelings into numbers. You could copy my method or invent your own, or your doctor may be able to provide you with a system. If you use mine, as it is or in a modified format, then you might be interested in constructing some blanks of the tables (shown as Tables I, 2, and 3, in the text) and initiate a procedure for filling them in on a daily basis. It only requires a few minutes and a bit of discipline each day. Calculations at the end of each week are demonstrated in the examples. You can then plot a point on your Chart 2 each week, or every six weeks after averaging, which was my approach. If you plot one point every week there may well be considerable fluctuations but you can always draw a best-fit line between them which will indicate the general direction. Do not worry if you appear to be going downhill now and again, you will get better in the end, (my Chart 2 oscillated quite violently before settling down). Show your doctor and keep plotting. Be fair to yourself and, above all, try to be consistent. Do not ever be over-optimistic or over-pessimistic. Your measurements should be as unbiassed as possible so that you end up with a true assessment of your condition. You are then in a better position to make an accurate choice of remedial treatment.

Chapter 8 – Once you can see your progress from your health records you can use them to decide what you might do to help yourself. I do not believe that it is possible to force depression any more than you can compel a broken limb to heal. You can assist the fracture by the correct combination of rest and then exercise, but you just have to wait for complete restoration. Likewise, the depression will go. You can help it on its way, but you cannot remove it by sheer willpower. Be as relaxed as you can about it. Your burden will lighten and eventually disappear. You may need to make some changes in your life, which you may not appreciate initially, but you cannot be in the position of damaging a broken limb every week, otherwise it will not mend. You may need to organise some stress-shredding exercises, which may require a very judicious selection of priorities. If you make a list of these, there can only be one at the top and this must be attended to before any of the others, even at the expense of some of the others. Be totally honest with yourself, take your time, get it right. Personally, when I have done my utmost myself, I 'inquire of the Lord' (as the scriptures advise), so that I can implement the course of action with confidence.

Chapter 9 – This is a general introduction to the use of this book as a 'workshop', self-help manual.

Chapter 10 – A long chapter which discusses sixteen specific ideas for you to try out. Those aspects which I deem to be essential are so indicated in the summary at the end of that chapter. Study each one carefully and add to them as appropriate. Decide in outline what you are going to do and make a start by writing something down. You will not get it all done today, but you can make a start today.

Chapter 11 – A few comments for the specific attention of those people who are anxious about somebody else suffering from stress. This chapter may also assist the patient in understanding the reactions of those around him (or her) who are trying to help.

Chapter 12 – This is where we are right now. If you feel that this book has been of help to you then read it again. Use it as a manual. Adapt it for yourself, for your condition, for your recovery. You can win through. I did, so you can. All the very best. JFH.